The Light of GOD'S Shadow

Musings, Stories and Poems on Waking Up

Jennifer (Jinks) Hoffmann

"Jinks Hoffmann sparkles. She radiates. Her impish wisdom, warm embrace of the full and fleeting adventure of the human condition, her childlike wonder and passionate devotion to both the unknowable Holy One and the holiness that lives and breathes between and among us, melt my heart. This collection of musings on mystical truths, parenting grown children and navigating life and death are essential for any spiritual director dedicated to celebrating the holy humanity of themselves and everyone they companion."

—**Mirabai Starr**
Author of *God of Love* and *Wild Mercy*

"Jinks 'had me' in the first lines of the Prologue. She described her discovery of the "secret of life" only to find it insufficient and in need of more searching. Through poetry, story-telling and deep vulnerable sharing of her life experiences we learn more about her continued searching. What each paragraph does is to invite us to reflect and continue our own searching. This is a book to keep on your nightstand and read again and again."

—**Lucy Abbott Tucker**
Former director of the Institute for Spiritual Leadership, Chicago, Founding Coordinating Council member, Spiritual Directors International, Author of *Spiritual Direction Supervision – Principles, Practices and Storytelling* (SDI Press)

"If you are looking for a guidebook to following your soul in these unprecedented times of crisis as well as in the ordinary moments of your daily life, look no further."

—**Diane M. Millis, PhD**
Author of *Re-Creating a Life*, *Deepening Engagement*, and *Conversation—the Sacred Art* (SDI Press)

"My friend Jinks Hoffmann has written an exquisite, inspired book of spiritual teaching, in prose and poetry, related to the teachings of six of her favorite teachers. She draws courageously on the darkest times of her life, when one can sometimes learn the most. Her wisdom is deep, loving and penetrating, both challenging and enticing."

—**Amy Eilberg**
Spiritual Director, Peace and Justice Educator, Teacher of Mussar and author of *From Enemy to Friend: Jewish Wisdom and the Pursuit of Peace*

"Savor Jennifer (Jinks) Hoffmann's poetry and prose as you "allow the light of God's shadow to shine" though you."

—**Rabbi Howard Avruhm Addison, PhD**
Associate Professor for Instruction, Temple University, Doctoral Studies Director in Jewish Spirituality, Graduate Theological Foundation, Co-editor of *Jewish Spiritual Direction* (Jewish Lights)

"This book is very timely, given the craziness we seem to be living through. It is my cup of tea. It grants space for the traditions to speak to one another and hits upon a key and healing part of the great tradition which needs reviving today — 'There be in God, some say, a deep but dazzling darkness.'"

—**Alan Jones OBE**
is an Episcopal priest and Dean Emeritus of Grace Cathedral in San Francisco.

"It took only 8 pages before my eyes filled with tears. It won't take you long to feel the intense desire to walk into your own "room" to wake up some more with a new soul friend."

—**Rabbi Phyllis Berman**
Mashpia (Spiritual Companion in the ALEPH Ordination Program and beyond), Meditator, Chanter, Swimmer, Baker, Savta, Midrash writer

"Using stories, poems, personal history, other peoples' history, varieties of religious experience, and the unsettling revelations of dreams, she speaks not from the pulpit but strolling right beside us, her arm tucked companionably into ours. Jinks brings to her elevated subject an enormous generosity of spirit, earthiness and humor, and her own special brand of irreverent reverence."

—**Judith Viorst**
Author of Necessary Losses, Alexander and the Horrible, Terrible, No Good, Very Bad Day, forty other books of prose and poetry for children and adults, and four musical plays.

"Reviewers sometimes write that they couldn't put a book down as if that's the greatest compliment. I *had* to put this exquisite book down, again and again, because it shimmers with a holy radiance that can only be absorbed a bit at a time. This book is a treasure."

—**Sandra Lommasson**
Mentor & Spiritual Director, Founder of the Sacramento-based Bread of Life Center, trainer of spiritual directors, soul-tender.

"This book is profoundly engaging and it uniquely opens our hearts and minds to embrace the light and shadow aspects of our selves so that we become more fully human. We are gifted with ageless gems of wisdom gleaned from the author's life experiences, insights from directees and inspirational poetry. Through the sacred bewilderment of laughter and tears, we slowly awaken to our higher self and begin to experience the mysterious glow of Presence."

—**Imam Jamal Rahman**
Co-founder of Interfaith Community Sanctuary and author of
Spiritual Gems of Islam

"*The Light of God's Shadow* does my heart good. With poetry and prose, Jinks Hoffmann writes undefended, inviting us to walk with her, savoring the bits and pieces of ordinary life, both the shadow and the light, benefited by her (positive) obsession with "*shmutz* cleaning". The result? She creates windows and doorways to gratitude, and living this day with a whole heart, the permission to fall in love with God once more."

—**Rev. Terry Hershey**
is a well-published author, humorist, inspirational speaker, dad, ordained minister, golf addict, and is smitten by French wine. He divides his time between designing sanctuary gardens and sharing his practice of mindfulness and savoring this life.

"In her wise and generous book, *The Light of God's Shadow*, Jinks Hoffmann makes the radically counter-cultural assertion that being in the rapids is not bad news. Lifting us with hope, while keeping us grounded in gritty truth, Jinks offers us a window into a life supported by connection to God and commitment to self-reflection."

—**Laura Goldman**
Teacher of Mussar and Jewish meditation, spiritual director, psychotherapist

The Light of GOD'S Shadow

Musings, Stories and Poems on Waking Up

Jennifer (Jinks) Hoffmann

2022

SDI Press
Bellevue, Washington, USA

Copyright © 2022 Jennifer (Jinks) Hoffmann

All rights reserved. No part of this publication may be reproduced in any form or by any means, electronic or mechanical, including photocopying, scanning, recording or by any information storage and retrieval system, without permission in writing from the publisher.

Brief quotations for reviews and articles about the publication are authorized.

Published by SDI Press, a division of Spiritual Directors International, 2025 112th Ave NE, Suite #200, Bellevue, WA 98004 USA.

www.sdicompanions.org
ISBN: 978-1-950309-05-4

Cover design: Matthew Whitney

Book layout: Ann Lancaster

Dedication

For Alan, Glen, Daniel, and Eli.

CONTENTS

Foreword 1
Entering: A Prologue 5
Chapter 1: Entering the Room 19
Chapter 2: Encountering Mystery 69
Chapter 3: Doing the Work 99
Chapter 4: Waking Up 133
Chapter 5: Encountering the Light 159
Chapter 6: Rediscovering That I'm Incurably Human 193
Chapter 7: Waking Up Again and Again 219
Chapter 8: Touching Unity: The Light of God's Darkness 249
Emerging: An Epilogue 287
Gifts from My Six 293
For Further Learning 313
Acknowledgements 317
About the Author 325

FOREWORD

In too much light there can be blindness, the ultimate darkness.

And in darkness, we can discover insight, the ultimate form of seeing.

These dichotomies and their interplay form the basis for this remarkable book, and its title, "The Light of God's Shadow." In it, Jinks Hoffmann shows us how our shadows point the way, and how the light can sometimes paradoxically lead us astray. Revealing that our expectations and assumptions are often upside down, with backwards forward, and forwards backward. So much so that we can find light and insight where we least expect it, and not at all where we most thought it might reside.

Through a wonderful combination of prose and poetry, Jinks talks about the terror and the "alarming blackness" she felt at various stages in her life, but particularly during the very turbulent and challenging last few years. Times where she often found herself sailing solo, with fear and horror at her back, through the infinite expanses of the universe. And yet, the light and darkness eventually conspired together to show her, and all of us, the way through.

A way that led from the alarm she initially felt at the darkness enveloping her, towards the unexpectedly soft and velvety blackness she eventually discovered. Showing us how our perspectives constantly shift. And then shift again, multivalently.

Jinks makes a compelling case that if we allowed ourselves to lean in to our shadows, we might come to quickly regard them as our ultimate companions, directors, and guides. They show us our failings in their rawest, most unadulterated forms, without blink or solace. They are direct and revealing, exposing trauma, anger, fear, uncertainty, and many other shortcomings that we need to address. And it's not as if we can avoid them in any event, because they don't allow us to run away for long, despite our best efforts.

Why not act in line with them instead, and align with them with the grace, compassion, warmth and tenderness that Jinks models in this book?

After all, shadows are not always harsh, and can be gentle, like those arising with the sun in the morning, or those in the evening, when it sets. At night, they comfort us as they become softly illuminated by candles and intertwine with wafting incense. And they encourage us as we start seeing beyond our hard edges, and move into the unknown with grace, acceptance and faith.

With Jinks at the helm, this work shows us that spiritual shadows, even as they usher in the often necessary dark night of our souls, are also the ultimate harbingers of light. At the bottom of a well of darkness, they light up the top of the universe. If we let them, they can profoundly and astutely guide us through our discomfort and pain, helping us work through our losses and fears, and towards Love and Compassion. Into the bosom of however we might conceive our transcendent immanence.

In Jinks' telling, The Shadow of God's Light thus become like compost to our spiritual flowering. It shows us what to process, and keeps pointing to what needs tending over and over again, as we slowly discern our way through heartbreak to growing insight and maturity. And as this book so well illustrates, our healing then takes root, and our shadows turn into fertilizers for our own spiritual journeys and ascendancies.

ENTERING: A PROLOGUE

Imagine this cartoon: On the left, several people wearing backpacks and climbing gear are scaling a very steep mountain. They are using ropes, crampons, T-nuts, harnesses, and iron chains. This is serious business. Some climb alone, others haul someone behind them. They are all clearly eager to reach the top where a faded sign reads THE SECRET OF LIFE. Imagine an old man on the right side of the cartoon. Clearly not visible to the climbers, he has a long beard and flowing robes—an archetypal guru. A bottle of hooch in one hand and a cigarette in the other, he whistles as he waits for the elevator that will whisk him to the top of the mountain.

I keep finding the secret of life. Each time, I am exultant. "This is really big," I tell my husband, Alan. "Now I know how to manage suffering, to feel joy most of the time, or, at the very least, equanimity." Alan smiles, a barely disguised "We've been here before" twinkle in his eyes.

As a psychotherapist and a spiritual director, I have had the gift and challenge of companioning souls for decades. As well, I have spent countless years honing spiritual practices and plugging away at my own personal work. All this time, deeply immersed in Jewish mysticism and Jungian psychology, I can now say one thing with confidence: Waking up is a lifetime's endeavor. I have learned through many years of successes and failures, of reaching pinnacles of consciousness and tumbling down rabbit holes, there is no secret to life, no way to create happily-ever-after. And who, at some primal, unconscious level, does not long for this? The work of waking up is painstakingly slow. Change in the psyche generally occurs more slowly than glacial melting. Perhaps even the enlightened are not conscious all the time. Yet waking up is my gig, the way I aspire to make my life as rich and purposeful as possible as I go about my blessed days. Perhaps some of my experiences will help you awaken more to the meaning and purpose of your own life.

I Walk into a Room

I have long been blessed with regular dreams in my sleeping life. Dreams, the unfolding stories of our souls, challenge us to wake up and follow our calling, our destiny. Almost always signposts on the road to healing and wholeness, some dreams may contain messages that suggest universal guidance. Dreams may also comment on the bread and butter of life. For example one of my dreams invited me to check whether our insurance policy covers massage. Until then, we had been paying out of pocket. "No way," said Alan, when I told him of the dream. "Check our insurance policy," I said. The dream was correct.

I believe that night dreams and unexpected thoughts with a distinctly "other" sensibility are examples of how the Source of Life points us toward becoming more conscious. Why consciousness? So we can help the Divine evolve, so we can lead intentional lives where we are more thoughtful and considerate. The final word, after all, is kindness—to others, to the planet, to ourselves. This dream, what Jung might have designated a big dream, is one I have been working with for years and will, for the rest of my life: *I walk into a room. I am suddenly, intensely awake. I think, "This is God." I feel terror. I feel wonder. I think "This is unity."*

This remarkable, mystical dream turned out to be prophetic and immeasurably valuable, as you will discover when you spend time with me in my room. As synchronicity—one way to talk about the Divine—would have it, when this book was coming together during the pandemic of 2020 and 2021, I was in my room, as were many of you. We were living through a horrific global crisis. My room, both concrete and metaphorical, evoked more awakening than I had ever imagined possible. Both psychological and spiritual growth are desirable in a life lived with the aim of consciousness. When we are awake, we experience intensely how extraordinarily wondrous life is—and how terrifying. We grow to know that a wholeness of life embraces a unity both dark and light, that God evokes both terror and wonder. My room—and here I'm not talking about the physical space—is the deep interior of my psyche, where I experience all of life with intensity. My room is my inner sanctum, where I am most awake to the Divine.

I Am Suddenly, Intensely Awake

For a period of almost two years, from mid 2019 to mid 2021, when my life journey was disrupted and stimulated by dramatic inner and outer events, I received what felt like a crash course in waking up: My teachers were COVID-19, the stark clarity of racial and social injustice, mounting disasters of climate change, the challenges of aging, colon cancer (my second cancer), and a new relationship with mortality. Early in this period I was set upon by a feeling of dread—anguish and frequently intense anxiety in my mind, heart, and body—unlike anything I had ever known. Brand-new and distinctly other, personal and existential, the foreboding was a master teacher. Four months later, it vanished. Finally, shockingly, in this two-year period, the worst thing any parent could possibly imagine occurred: Our son Eli died.

As wretched as this long period was, I knew that I had no choice but to stay in my room, to wake up and be intensely present, to be alive to the dark and light of life and of Ultimate Reality. I had no choice but to keep asking of the Holy One, "What now, my Love?" for perhaps our breath, our discernment, and our love are all we have in the final analysis.

This book is a collection of candid and colorful musings on waking up when we are in big trouble. The ideal, of course, is to be awake all the time, although we know this is impossible. It is important, too, to follow our souls, our energy in ordinary moments, not just in times of crisis. Do we go into the garden to deadhead the irises, or read lofty material, then meditate and write? "What shall we do now, Holy One?" we may ask. This sweet dailyness of connection with the Divine is somewhat different from when we are gasping for breath. Being awake is the goal.

I Think, "This Is God"

I have been in my room many times over the course of my life. When deeply connected to soul, everything is intensely vivid, and the invitation to consciousness unmistakable. I know it is cheeky to talk as if I know anything about the Ineffable. But frankly, I can't help it. Most of us talk endlessly about what we love. Life happens, sometimes in ways that threaten to unmoor us. And yet as devastating as any moment might be, we can choose not to be a victim. There is always, at every moment of the eternal now, an invitation to discernment, a potential for deeper awakening. We ask the Beloved, "How do I manage this? What am I to learn here? How can I grow?" We listen, look around to the environment for clues, plumb our depths for answers. We read, we write, we pray. We ask our dreams to talk with us. We may discern nothing. Yet just the questions, inviting engagement with the Holy, are valuable and empowering. Even when we think we have some answer to a question, we can never be sure it's God talking. But still we ask. Even more, we commit ourselves to the questions. The musings, stories, and poems that follow, drawn from my most recent abiding in my inner sanctum of deepest connection, are intended to inspire you to ask your own questions and engage more deeply with the light and dark shadow of life and the Divine.

Why bother doing the spiritual and psychological work that brings you face-to-face with yourself and the totality of life—goodness, evil, abundance, scarcity, darkness, light, love? If we're awake, we know we are in the presence of the Source of Life, the Holy. We know that darkness and light are of the One, that life is both terrifying and wondrous. We touch the inescapable reality that we are not in control, that every moment of life is uncertain, unpredictable, that existence is a blessed gift. As we learn more about the ongoing nature of awakening, as we repeatedly listen, we may hear the Divine speak from deeper levels of consciousness. We become more conscious that the journey undertaken by our own divine spark is the key to living in relationship with life's holiness. Knowing that each moment is sacred, we recognize the urgent call to kindness and compassion—for others, for ourselves, for all creatures, for the earth. Why bother to wake up? Because waking up to ourselves, all of life and the Divine is the doorway to love in action.

When awake, our loving-kindness is balanced by the power of firmness, and living becomes more mindful, our choices clearer, and frequently more beautiful. Mysticism teaches that the Divine, like us, is in an ongoing process of evolution. It is inspiring and humbling to realize that doing our personal work can be part of the solution to the ills of the world. Implanted in each of us is a call to share what we learn from the Holy One. I believe that what I cheerfully call "*shmutz* [mess] cleaning," which is deep psychospiritual work, may be among our most sacred work. Our son Daniel, who is both a social worker and an organic farmer, is fond of saying, "From one seed an entire orchard can grow. So, I shall be the healthiest seed I can be." *Tikkun ha-nefesh* (healing of the soul) in the service of *tikkun ha-olam* (healing of the world) is one of the holiest and most urgent invitations from life. When the unresolved "stuff" of our childhood runs our life, our blessed wounds can make a mess. There may be nothing more important than becoming aware of this, tending ourselves lovingly, and cleaning up the mess we make. Each period of deep work brings us closer to our wholeness, to the Transcendent One. We also learn, over and over again, that our wounds are our wounds and that there is no squeaky clean. We come to know that a "cure" may simply be the swifter awakening to the fact that we have fallen, once more, into a *shmutz* trap.

We'd all like to think that our waking up will be linear—that how awake we feel today is how awake we'll be tomorrow, and on and on we will grow. But that's not how waking up works. Waking up will take us up and down, left and right, into and out of both light and darkness—sometimes all in one day and certainly over our weeks and months and years. Similarly, the stories, musings, and poems that follow are not linear. As you read, you may notice that in one moment I grumble about the vagaries of aging, and several chapters later I write about being a child growing up in South Africa. You will observe that

Entering: A Prologue

I am a spiritual director before I train to become one. You will discover that my colon cancer is gone, yet later will accompany me as I experience radiation and chemotherapy. And so on. The musings, stories, and poems do not follow a sequence in time but make their own decisions about where to appear in the book. This way of viewing life is consistent with a teaching in Jewish mysticism, where the past, present, and future all exist simultaneously. I find this perspective inexpressibly moving, enriching, inspiring. When we enter the room where we are suddenly intensely awake and know that everything is God, we can suspend our usual way of thinking. We can celebrate that life does not have to be neat, orderly, predictable. We can enter a world where time does what it will, where children, donkey drivers, and pandemics are often wisdom teachers, where we have a hand in shaping the future, which, like the past, is occurring now.

Please, thus, enter this book at any place, at any moment. Hang out with yourself and with me wherever you are spiritually in the moment. In your own life, for example, you may become disconcerted because right after feeling decidedly enlightened, you find that you are the proverbial neophyte, tied in knots once more. Your aged father is cranky and unreasonable, has begun smoking, and insists on driving to the doctor—alone. Your dad is your dad. What can *you* do to feel aligned once more with your wholeness, to be kind to your father and yourself? The invitation in chapter 7 to wake up some more may be just the ticket for you. Meander. Wander around in my room. Trust your soul, your energy, to guide you. You may notice that I say some things over and over again. Our things are our things, and my passions have a way of repeating themselves. You may become aware that there are contradictions in my story. I sometimes say one thing and then—somewhat unapologetically—its opposite. That's mysticism for you. It's beautiful if we don't fight it.

I Feel Terror. I Feel Wonder

After dinner on the final night of Chanukah in December 2020, Alan and I watched the colored candles as they burned down. The light was soft and comforting, even though we had just been speaking about Eli for the hundredth time that day. Eli, our oldest son, was just fifty-two when he died of advanced liver disease. He had been number one on the liver transplant list in Israel. Tragically, his liver began failing before a donor became available, and while he fought valiantly for ten days, surprising the doctors every single day by his will to live, he did not make it. Eli was father to fifteen remarkable children and eleven grandchildren. The twelfth grandchild, a boy, was born fairly soon after Eli died. The new baby was blessed to receive Eli's name—Eliyahu Yonatan—at his bris (circumcision ceremony). Alan and I were present on Zoom (God help us) for the ceremony in Israel. We wept with sorrow and also joy. Eli and Ilana, his remarkable wife, created a tribe where all is met with enthusiasm and a life-giving vitality. Even Eli's death has not crushed the spirit in the family. Eli was loved by countless before and after his death. He inspired many to become their very best selves.

Strangely, I was blessed by one of my dream oracles around this time, an incomplete sentence that said: *The light of God's darkness.* The compelling dream offered some hope. The day after Chanukah ended, I walked with the Divine, praying, listening, touching my place of silence. The loss of our son, rising numbers of COVID-19 deaths and infections, nasty weather, the impossibility of being with our family in Israel or even hugging our Canadian family, combined to make me utterly miserable. "Where is the light of your darkness now?" I grumbled to the Holy One. Scared by reports of a more virulent strain of the virus, lost in thought, I trudged through puddles of melted, muddy snow and kept crossing the road anxiously to avoid other walkers.

It took only one person. A small woman, being pulled along by a huge Great Dane, caroled cheerfully, "Who do you think is boss here?" from the other side of the road. When I laughed, she went on to say, "Hang in, friend. We can do it." Suddenly, intensely awake, I was in the light of God's darkness. And as we went our separate ways, I became aware of the strange beauty of a naked mulberry tree, its sturdy, dark branches reaching out like open arms. Feeling a gentle, loving sorrow about Eli, I was flooded with compassion for all of us who are managing life during these dark and occasionally wondrous days. When I am wide awake and present, I am in my body, vibrantly engaged with life. I almost always feel wonder, compassion, and tenderness. Open to the light of God's darkness, I witness spirit, even in trees, stark, dark, naked, and open. I see the beauty of our son, after his death, even more than I did when he was alive.

As you enter this grounded and mystical world of musings, stories, and poems, you will accompany me during the most challenging time of my life, when despair often felt like ground glass in my mouth, and I frequently could not find a soft place. As COVID-19 tore through the world, I connected regularly with my friend David, who works as a chaplain and the administrator in a Christian eldercare home. Many of the people he had come to love were dying because of COVID-19. "Still in your room?" I wrote each time in the subject line. "Still here," David replied. I kept at it, too, working my stuff, asking to learn from life and my blessed wounds, praying for compassion. Dave and I frequently wanted to pull the darkness of this time around us, shut our eyes, opt out. But anguish will take us deeper into ourselves if we let it. Then, as we descend into emptiness, we may be better able to enter the realm of mystery. The extent to which we can companion our pain or fear may be the extent to which we can meet the light, the incalculable radiance, the spark of God's light in the impenetrable darkness. The extent to which we engage with life, eyes wide open, may allow us to savor the unity of the Holy. Ever aware that existence is a Rorschach blot seen through the eyes of our own projections, and equally aware of the fleeting nature of reality, we nonetheless try to find our truth in the forever transforming now, so we can be present in the moment and extract the essence of what life has delivered to us. This is the alchemy of our reality. This is God. Even if it is the unspeakable tragedy of losing a son.

I Think, "This Is Unity"

Writing poetry is one of the ways I talk with and listen to my heart, to life, and to God. My dreams are frequently brief and explicit. One told me, *You are to write poems in response to the prose of others.* Some years after this dream, I found myself in the midst of an exciting writing project—poetry in response to the inspiring teachings of six writers of contemporary Jewish mysticism—Arthur Green, Melila Hellner-Eshed, Michael Fishbane, Lawrence Kushner, Tirzah Firestone, and Sanford Drob. Their prose elicited my poems—call and response. I did not realize that the poems were clustered around this remarkable group of people until I found the courage to seek out and connect with Michael Fishbane. I told him about my adventure and mentioned the others to whom I was responding. "Ah," he said, "a chorus of voices." Michael then reported that some of my six, as I have come to call them, had been close friends since their early days as rabbis, writers, or teachers. Almost all knew one another. How wondrous.

When I began my project, I imagined that I would write a nice little book of poetry as a paean to my six, about God and life and love and sorrow and fresh almond butter and cherry jam on twelve-grain toast. But life—in mainly very nasty ways—intervened, and the Boss, as I sometimes call the Beloved, seemed to want me to go in a somewhat different direction. Although I could have written tomes of poems about all I learned from my teachers, it was as if I were being told to scrap any plans I had, settle in for the long haul ahead, and listen for what I was being taught. At the same time, I was to turn to the guidance and wisdom of my six to help me through the worst crisis of my life. *Not only poems but also prose*, it seems I was being told.

My six all have their own ways of thinking, feeling, and writing about the Divine and mysticism. In every single poem in this book, you will meet one of these teachers by way of an epigraph that holds a mirror to one of their remarkable souls. The poem that follows each epigraph is a love letter describing different ways of perceiving and experiencing the Holy One, in ordinary and extraordinary life. You'll learn more about these wonderful teachers in "Gifts from My Six."

I have spent many years with my six, first thing every morning when still close to the world of dreams and my unconscious. Their soulful reflections and uniquely different perspectives on Jewish theology and mysticism frequently call forth my "God-tears." That's what happens when I awaken to God's face: I am stopped by an emotion, an insight, a challenge. I know I am to write when tears occur, when I salivate, have goose bumps, or feel heat in my body. My body-soul is saying, "Stop. Be here now. Listen in. Write." I pause and put the book aside to allow a poem to arrive. "What, Beloved? Talk to me in my thoughts, through my heart." We can intuit the Divine through our learning and our thoughts, in our lives, bodies, and hearts, in our souls and dreams, and through the great spirit of grace.

Invitation to You

Bev and I are doing a Zoom session. A single mother with two late-teen kids, she is a nurse who works in a large downtown hospital. Bev is one of the "lifers" I companion, someone who knows that becoming conscious and engaging in spiritual growth are a lifetime's commitment. Toward the end of our time, Bev asks why I have been working on myself for over forty years. "I think it's for three reasons," I say. "To keep waking up. So I can make choices from a place of consciousness. To be kinder."

Bev thinks a while, then says, "Yes. And there's something more. It's almost political. When I meditate at home alone, perhaps I am doing something that is not just for myself, but something that may benefit the world." "Radical mindfulness?" I wonder aloud. Deep personal work often leads people to turn their eyes and hearts outward. Bev is on fire now: "Before meditating I am often just too exhausted to do anything but stare at my cat. Afterward, I have energy to go across the road and mow my elderly neighbor's lawn, clean her yard. I must say, though"—Bev does that thing with her eyebrows—"I so look forward to meeting in person. Zoom is a radical pain."

I had another big dream that told me, *You are to row alone to an island. On God's holy day, the thirteenth. To plant seeds of uncertainty and unknowing.* This directive to plant seeds of uncertainty and unknowing, not just once, but countless times, tells us that waking up is a forever project. When we are awake and conscious, we can make choices that are kind, that include others. Seeds, when planted and tended mindfully, bear fruit.

Enter my room with me and your own inner sanctum, where, naked and vulnerable in our authenticity, we can speak from within—not about—our lives. When we ask for moment-to-moment guidance from the Great Creator we learn more about ways to awaken, to glimpse the unity. Now, with more faith in entering the dark, we receive and embrace the light of God's darkness. Here we find harsh loneliness, the cruelty of nature, the biting entanglements of human relationships, the cold abyss of grief, mystery that can terrify. We also find unspeakable beauty, the blaze of love and community, the uplift in awe, creativity, and the Breath of Life on our cheeks. We find the courage to love, and love more, to allow the light of God's Shadow to shine through us.

CHAPTER 1: ENTERING THE ROOM

Wile E. Coyote and the Roadrunner

The holier the event, the more ways it can be retold.
—Lawrence Kushner, *Kabbalah: A Love Story*

I'm terrified
that if
I stop
racing

to overthrow
and defeat
my nemesis

I will find
I am
Wile E. Coyote

legs pedaling
furiously
atop
the abyss.

I need
to remember
I will never
catch

the Roadrunner.

Furthermore
I've already

fallen.

Chapter 1: Entering the Room

The Time of Dread

In my seventy-seventh year, when this book was starting to come together, I experienced the darkest and most translucent four months of my life. It started suddenly. One afternoon when I lay down for my customary post-lunch nap, I could not fall asleep. I felt dread—a darkness unlike anything I had ever known. Shocked and bewildered, I looked around in terror. I had known anxiety that is stomach-kicking and ugly, and still do at times. This was of a different order—dark distress that was intensely visceral, as if something did not belong. I wondered if it were me.

Over this period of four months, feelings of terror, which almost never made any sense, came, and went. Having worked on waking up for forty years or more, I trust that I am mostly solid and grounded spiritually and psychologically. However, in this seemingly interminable period, I could no longer count on any sustained sense of safety or the loving presence of the Holy. It seemed that God's eyes of love were closed to me. Mostly, I only sensed darkness. In the early days of the "time of dread," as I began to think of it, I felt shame. I worked hard to preserve my persona, but berating and cajoling myself had absolutely no impact. Eventually, my hubris was wrestled to the ground. I tucked my self-image in the bottom of my underwear drawer and prayed fervently to accept my unfamiliar shakiness, perhaps even to understand what was happening. Even more, I prayed for the terrible dread to pass.

I had walked into my room. Others may enter their rooms by choice. I don't. Crisis is what usually kicks me in.

During these life-changing months I was immensely grateful for brief, unexpected moments of awe and wonder that leavened the dread: The ever-changing landscape of natural life in the bone-cold of winter. The sweet warmth of strangers. A moment on television where a big dog and toddler were eye to eye. My work as a spiritual companion, in which I am frequently moved to tears by the courage of my people to plumb their depths. Alan's unceasing kindness in listening to my anguish. (I talk a lot.) I was once more in my room and had become intensely awake. I knew from my immersion in my beloved Jewish mysticism that an experience of the Divine that surrounds and fills all worlds is an experience of Oneness. I knew that there is nothing but God. But this knowing was in my head. In my body and heart, I mainly felt terror.

Life occurs around and within us. We pay attention and learn from reality, or don't. I believe that if we're awake, we feel all life as sacred and know that everything is God. We intuit the unity of the Divine, the light and the dark. We know that plumbing our unfathomable depths and asking "What now?" of our deepest wisdom may offer guidance and comfort. In my time of dread, what I knew mostly was confusion and fear. Although I never lost my faith in the existence and presence of the Holy One, or my belief that the Divine is in large part loving, I had no way to connect with the light of God, to feel the breath of the Great Creator on my face. The dark night felt interminable. I wondered if I was meeting God's dark shadow. It seemed that the Divine was saying, "Kid, we have some work to do. Let's go."

Our souls are shaped by a multitude of forces. Among these are our own ordinary psychological stories in all their rich complexity; the spiritual, existential actuality we live in every single moment; and the possible ancestral traumas that are unwittingly passed down from generation to generation. Reality is a shape shifter, and any attempts to control life are like trying to grasp at air as we plummet in free fall.

My time of dread was occasioned in part by psychological wounds. In my childhood, my unhappiness or anxiety made my father unhappy and anxious. As a young child I learned to banish my darker feelings. I worked hard to be happy and at ease, so my father would be comfortable. This was perhaps my central organizing story. As children, we learn strategies to keep us safe. Our defenses against the small or large traumas make our realities more manageable. There is no way to overstate how these very defenses, which served us so well as children, may keep us from living rich and textured lives as adults. And, oh, the terror when life calls us to dismantle our familiar ways of feeling safe. I became aware, as a young woman, about my "Anxiety is dangerous" complex. My work was cut out for me. As I aged, I continued from time to time to fall back into the uh-oh feeling whenever I felt anxious. However, the more I grew in consciousness, the less I became trapped in uh-oh. Jungians believe that we are "cured" when we become familiar with our complexes and learn to show them the door pretty smartly when they appear, as they inevitably will. A complex, simply put, is an array of emotions that are excessive to the reality of the moment. Complexes almost always have their origins in the wounds of our early lives. We all have complexes. Complexes may be both positive and negative. Overwhelming happiness can also sometimes be forced and not entirely from our healthy place.

My dread was also a response to spiritual and existential truths. I prayed to accept the growing terror and pain of *truly* knowing I cannot know God. I prayed to absorb in my bones that the Divine, not I, was running the show. I was not in control of whether I could fall asleep at night any more than

I could be the boss over whether Alan, or any of my children, stayed alive. Being awake in our bodies to the randomness of existence, where we are at the mercy of life, of Creator God, is terrifying. Buddhist teachings challenge us to come to terms with the reality that the ground beneath our feet is forever shifting. There is not much but our breath to count on. If we really know this, we might feel terror. God the boss is decidedly less attractive to me than God the beloved, whose love feels immediate, visceral, almost overwhelming. My God, like the Divine of the mystical worlds, has plenty of names.

My dread may also have been a response to some familial wound in my parents, their parents, or their parents' parents. My family of origin all knew the secret that my father was highly anxious and that his father probably was, too. But why and what it meant for me in my soul, in my body, I did not know. I learned, only when I was seventy-eight, that my maternal grandparents had lost Joseph, their baby boy, to scarlet fever. My mother, the youngest of five girls, never spoke of this and apparently neither did anyone else.

There was much going on in my dear body, mind, heart, soul. Sometimes, if we are fortunate, our psyche brings forward the stuff we need to explore—ways in which our past wounds and conflicts, present longings, and unfulfilled needs cry out for tender attention. Sometimes we are taken deeper into knowing the unknowability of the Holy One, and the randomness of life's unfolding. This, although seldom an elegant experience, can be life-changing and even magnificent.

This archetypal consciousness, which felt distinctly other, departed as suddenly and dramatically as it had arrived four months before. Two weeks later I was diagnosed with colon cancer.

Annus Horribilis and Longer

Chemotherapy and radiation began soon after my diagnosis of colon cancer and lasted for five weeks. An outbreak of the novel coronavirus that had begun to manifest in the world as a pandemic showed up in North America in late February 2020. In April 2020, a day after my seventy-seventh birthday, I entered the hospital for surgery. Alan drove me there. We kissed goodbye. I opened the car door and walked into the hospital alone, forlorn, and anxious, as I pulled my overnight case behind me. No family member could visit for the three days of my stay. I was in darkness, alone. A rehearsal for my death.

Just one month later, in May 2020, George Floyd was murdered and the Black Lives Matter movement erupted internationally. As the year staggered on doggedly, the world fractured daily. Societal injustice and systemic racism were visible as never before. Our dread amplified as COVID-19 began to sweep the globe. We grieved about the political upheaval of this time, the emergence of the far right, the horrors wrought by climate change. We were being asked to witness the weeping of the soul of the world, to take action and reduce the violence enacted daily upon others and on our beloved earth. We were being called on to engage in acts of *tikkun ha-nefesh* in the service of *tikkun ha-olam*—the healing of our souls in the service of the healing of the world. "How can we serve You at this time in the eternal now?" we were to ask, over and over again.

As the scourge of COVID-19 swept the planet, we became more aware of our interconnectedness, of how profoundly we are our brothers' and sisters' keepers. To potentially save lives, we needed to stay in our homes unless we were essential workers. All of us were to wear masks and keep distant from one another. Yet these days and months of darkness were often punctuated by people's kindness and generosity. Because we were not able to be near one another, friends and family left homemade soup and muffins at the front doors of friends and family. People listened endlessly to each other's tales of this new and frightening world, on Zoom, Skype, and phone calls, on face time and on emails. Community, although virtual, in some cases became stronger.

In these strange and numinous days of darkness and light, I turned more urgently toward my six—my guides into the world of Jewish mysticism—and heard their call with renewed urgency: We must come closer to the One, the Source of Life. Awareness of the blessed sacredness of life usually evokes increasing kindness and responsibility toward others and our earth. The life we had known was disappearing. I fiercely missed hugging our Canadian family and my friends, and although my own sorrows paled in comparison to the thought of people dying alone, I held my own grief tenderly—most of the time. Many of us felt we were being invited to live with the terror and awe that this time in history stirred in us. We prayed to be transformed ourselves and to transform the world. Perhaps we were being asked to turn and face our own darkness and that of the Divine—to be in our hearts, our bodies, to stay with our grief, our rage, our confusion until we could discern the light of God's darkness.

The COVID-19 catastrophe grew more frightening. Alan and I learned to adjust, at least somewhat. And then the unthinkable— our oldest son, Eli, began to deteriorate from the nonalcohol cirrhosis he had had for over twenty years. We had known about Eli's condition forever, it seemed, and that "someday" a liver transplant was a long shot. But in August 2020 Eli became ill and his liver began to fail. Eli was number one in Israel for a transplant, and while we were all anxious, we had confidence a liver donor would materialize. After all, it was Eli. He could do anything. In late October, Eli entered the hospital in Jerusalem and for ten intolerable days he fought for his life. An invitation to stay with the darkness of life came as never before, when our beloved Eli died on November 4, 2020.

Everything and Nothing

The Kabbalists held Ein-sof, the "infinite God," to be everything and nothing, the object of all the attributes and completely ineffable and unknowable.
—Sanford Drob, *Jungian Psychology and the Challenge of Contemporary Atheism*

I've been talking about God
since—at six—I first heard
Moonlight Sonata.
There's both
everything
and nothing
    to say.
It is simply
foolish

to open my mouth
one
more
time.
Yet I do.
    Oh mercy, I do.

Just as foolish
to talk,
weep—yet one
more time—about COVID's stark
isolation, cancer's brutal
chemo treatment, about

learning
to poop
again.

But I never learn.
So, I say
everything.
   Every
      little
         thing.
And I weep.
     Oh mercy, I do.

And my sweetheart,
drenched—yet one more
time—by tears
about God and cancer,
smiles kindly and thinks:
She's saying nothing

new.
Yet look: Everything
is illuminated. The sun
has just come from behind
the clouds.

My Awakening Began with Anxiety

If you ever asked my mother-in-law how she was, you would get a weather report. "It's windy," she would say, "and they are talking about rain." Ask many in the psychotherapy field how they are and you will get a rundown of their emotional state. My primary language is that of the heart.

At thirty-three, when I returned to Canada from my father's funeral in South Africa in 1976, I experienced an enormous amount of grief and intense anxiety. There is grief, and there is grief that is so immense it can alert us to some tangled knot in our psyches. As it turned out, immediately after my return, I entered a four-year training program at the Gestalt Institute of Toronto to become a psychotherapist. Anxiety, sometimes an SOS from the deep, can be a symptom of our unresolved stuff, the large or small traumas of our childhoods. In the training program, we called this "unfinished business." Our training required us to dive deeply into the ways our wounds manifested as *shmutz*. The person who was "working" would sit in the hot seat, which was a pillow in those days of the '70s. With the help of the group leader, and the support of the group, I explored my anxiety in several "sits" in the hot seat. I began to recognize some of my interior pain, conflict, confusion, anger, and the longings that I could not have recognized or managed as a child. Healing is furthered when, as adults, we pay deep attention to our hearts, thoughts, and bodies. When we enter the field of pain, confusion, and anger, we allow our unconscious to teach us and possibly transform us. Some believe that the unconscious is one of God's favorite hiding places.

As students, we learned that no one goes into therapy unless they are in pain, that becoming aware is a lifetime's opus. In those Gestalt days, I was heady with the excitement of learning how our neuroses can keep us from being authentically present in the here and now. I learned, too, that the process of psychological healing mirrors awakening to the Divine. As we become familiar with some of our *shmutz*—a process that is repeated for the rest of our lives—we become more awake to wonder and awe, terror, and darkness.

There are countless ways it is possible to journey to the center of the heart. There are also infinite ways to awaken to the fact that we are not driving the bus. Life shows us who we are in the mirror of reality if we have the courage to look. As Dietrich Bonhoeffer wrote, "Our brother breaks the circle of self-deception." We learn to have compassion as we discover how our unhealed wounds sometimes show up as confused or sticky behavior, thoughts, or emotions. In the realm of the psychospiritual, this is some of the most holy work we can do. If we do, we may learn to exit a little more quickly from our particular morass of unconsciousness, and to be kinder to ourselves and others.

When I returned from South Africa, the unfinished business from my childhood and the possible intergenerational trauma in my psyche threw me into a state of acute anxiety and chaos. I felt profoundly alone in the darkness, with barely an experience of God. But if we want to stay intensely alive, we need to turn toward the dark, which can be very arduous and painful work.

Almost Too Much

For Judaism all things—including garbage, sweat, dirt and bushes—are not impediments to, but dimensions of spirituality.
—Lawrence Kushner, God Was in This Place, & I, i Did Not Know

Rod Stewart's gravelly voice
fills the car—
It's over...
all the pain and all
the grievin'—

She taps the steering wheel,
bum-dances in the seat.
Admires her sexiness.

She stops

at a traffic light,
watches a teen
in a school uniform
consult
his phone.

She hears him
laugh
as he pulls on backward
a navy toque.

Chapter 1: Entering the Room

A few autumn leaves
still blaze—

throbbing reds
and yellows,
curling inward.

It is almost too much—
life, today—
trumpeting
celebration.
Almost
too much.

She shuts off

the radio.
A sudden need
for quiet, to study

the air,
her thoughts,
the way
this day
blesses her.

She drives, slowly,
now
with reluctance,
toward
the house of

The Light of God's Shadow

    her friend
    who, after a botched

heart
operation,
no longer,
    no longer
        has legs.

Chapter 1: Entering the Room

I Feel You

 Alan and I discovered the acclaimed TV series *The Wire* rather late in the game, and we became instantly addicted to the archetypal story line and characters. Despite the fact that I often had to read the commentary after each episode for clarification, we soon understood why it was Barack Obama's favorite show. The gritty series—a dramatized Dickensian novel in a sense—is about Baltimore cops, drug lords, and wiretaps. It is starkly realistic, painful, profound. There are very few good guys. Yet, strangely, it was in this dark series that I first heard the phrase "I feel you" and suddenly understood what happened when things were right between the Holy One and me, when I was in alignment. God, for me, is an experience, not an idea. When I could not feel the One, I suffered.

 I am writing this on February 24, 2020, the day that a guilty verdict was delivered to Harvey Weinstein for rape and sexual assault. The #MeToo movement declared a victory. It is the same day that many, their hearts suddenly broken, spoke in disbelief about the revelations of sexual abuse that had just been made public about Jean Vanier. Vanier, the son of a Canadian diplomat and governor general, had declared that he wanted to follow Jesus when he first founded L'Arche (The Ark) in 1963. He provided communities for people with learning disabilities to live as equals alongside those without disability. Today there are 153 L'Arche communities in thirty-eight countries on five continents. Vanier, who it is rumored was being considered for sainthood and the Nobel Peace Prize, persuaded his female spiritual directees to be sexually engaged with him, claiming mystical and spiritual beliefs as justification. How do we manage our enormous shock and sorrow about the dark shadows cast by those who also have shone such a great light?

In the psychospiritual realm, everybody suffers. To be born means you will suffer. Buddhist teachings invite us to learn that pain is inevitable, suffering optional. I am a big fan of the whole Buddhist perspective on nonattachment, which calls on us not to cling to happiness or try to push away misery but rather to live with whatever life dishes up with as much equanimity as possible. But despite all the inner work, over many more years than the Israelites wandered the desert, I have as yet no reliable way to control or stop my suffering. "Pain is inevitable, suffering optional" are undeniably excellent words, yet for me there also is suffering that is pure and healthy, and not something we should try and change by having a different attitude. Each time I receive another lesson in awakening, whether a brief lesson, such as an afternoon and early evening of hell, my four-month time of dread, or the long study of my two-year period where too much felt almost intolerable, I learn this fact anew. When I cannot feel God's presence, I have no felt sense of being companioned and loved. Then I am in big trouble. I am suffering.

Chapter 1: Entering the Room

The Orchid

[Pay] close attention to what's going on inside and [accept] whatever arises with compassion.
—Tirzah Firestone, Wounds into Blessings

Thank You
for the loan
of this body
and this time
on earth, though
I must confess
I am not crazy
about *all* of it.

I know my task
is to meet
the cancer just
as I do
the orchid
on the windowsill
in the kitchen
that gets
the morning sun
and is close
to blooming
a second
time. But
some things—
even You
must admit—

are less
enchanting
than others.

Thank You
anyway
for Your patience
with my lack
of *same*,
for this morning's
breath
for this body
that moves
with anticipation
toward
seventy-seven.

I know
I am not
supposed
to hope and all,
just meet
everything
with equanimity,
so thanks
for Your
broad-mindedness.

And while
I have Your
attention,

Chapter 1: Entering the Room

could we
aim, please,
for eighty
or even more?
And would You please
remember
I am still
a student
at life?

And can
that bloody orchid
bloom already?

Pain and Suffering

Most of us have our own laundry list of suffering. My pain and lack of control in the repeated expansions and contractions in the birth and delivery of our three sons could have been the physical presage to the grief we knew when our boys struggled, as children inevitably do, with anxieties, anger, difficulties at school, feelings of being different, a religious conversion. The many ways Alan and I—such imperfect parents—wounded and created pain in our sons is something we have blessedly talked about with all of them—several times.

We could never have imagined we would lose our oldest son at fifty-two. There are simply no words for this heartbreak.

There were two periods in our marriage so fraught with struggle and pain that Alan and I both feared that the end of our marriage was possible. The possibility of life without Alan was even more alarming to me than the time I had breast cancer. I remember walking the roads of our neighborhood wishing I were dead. In those dark days I wept and felt great fear, but I did not feel alone. I did not feel the agony of God's absence. I was in pain but I was not trapped in unbearable suffering, for I was grounded in a love that was bigger than me. Blessedly, Alan's and my innate attachment and profound love served as glue during those times and we were able to survive our crises, learn from our messes, and ultimately enrich our love with greater consciousness and tenderness. Crisis can be mulch for continuing growth and love.

I lost two close women friends well before their time: Merle died of cancer in her early forties, and Brenda was hit by a truck as she ran across a road. Our friend Stan died recently—Alan's closest friend for seventy-six years. I stop to feel my pain as I write: I still miss them all. At the time, Merle asked how I felt about her approaching death. "Basically, ghastly. Thank you for asking." I wept. "I know," she said, taking my hands. She paused for a while and then whispered, "You are going to just lose me. I am going to lose everyone."

In these later years of our lives, Alan and I speak frequently of our less-than-agile navigation of life, our physical pain, the diminishments that accrue with aging. These losses are the subject of many of the conversations we have with each other and our friends. "Organ recitals," we sometimes joke. Our children witness us a little reduced and don't much like it, just as we felt when our own parents aged and then died.

I do not like pain, but I am able to feel it. I can be in my heart and my body. I can cry and grieve without shame. I trust sorrow and allow it to lead me out of the thicket when it has received its full due. To paraphrase the poet Robert Frost, the best way out is through. My suffering, though, without connection to another or to my felt sense of life's sacred, is of a different order. My theology, always in process and grounded in Jewish mysticism and Jungian psychology, holds that there is a Oneness. Everything is God, *Ein Sof*, the infinite—both/and, light and dark, a glorious and sometimes hideous totality. The Divine is a comingling of all that is possible: the pod of at least twenty dolphins frolicking just off the shore outside our winter home; our granddaughter Clara, who at age nine is sewing sweatpants and beanbags; my friend Diane, whose jazzy imagination and deep theological passion enlivens and enriches our monthly sharing of our creative endeavors. Creator God is the one drop of dew visible on the just blooming yellow hibiscus on the deck, and also Jean Vanier, Harvey Weinstein, and our friend Lin, who lost both her legs in a heart operation that went shockingly wrong.

I believe that at every moment in the history of the world, there is an urgent call to humanity: We need to be still enough to know God's darkness and our own. Our darkness can be the healthy pain that longs for loving attention as much as the darkness of our own unconscious psyche. When we meet the dark shadow in ourselves, through our dreams and the ways in which life and people hold a mirror to us, we can more easily contain our entitled, selfish, judgmental impulses. We become familiar with our shadow, nod kindly to it, and behave with decency. Then we can forgive our less-than-perfect humanity, and feel compassion for the whole human race, including ourselves. Perhaps we can even intuit the aspect of divinity that is pure love, compassion, forgiveness. The light of the shadow of the Divine.

We Cannot Change the Past—We Can Only Change Our Feelings about It

When I was a psychotherapist, I worked with Eliza, whose specialty was family law. She was smart and funny and had a gift for seeing the sweetness in life. Her energy and creativity were prodigious. Eliza had a rambunctious boy of seven and was a good mother to her son—most of the time, she said. Everything was good, she declared in our first session, except for her problem—her brother, Jeff. Eliza was an example of how we can sometimes avoid profound pain by creating neurotic suffering. I use the word *neurotic* with kindness and affection. Jung taught that our neuroses are flags waving from our unconscious, requesting healing.

Jeff was a highly successful Supreme Court judge. No

matter how Eliza tried to create a close relationship with him, Jeff was cold and distant, polite but uninterested. Birthday cards, Christmas gifts, phone calls inviting Jeff and his wife to lunch and dinner elicited little response. Eliza understood that her brother reminded her of their alcoholic, angry father, but she was more interested in trying to involve me in diagnosing Jeff psychologically than in talking about her dad. Although she did not know this, what was mostly operative was that Eliza did not want to experience any of the feelings she had had as a sad, angry, helpless girl.

Several months of therapy ensued. Eliza continued to obsess about Jeff. My efforts to help her be in her body and connect with her emotions were met with clever defenses. She simply could not accept the painful reality of her inability to transform Jeff. One day, however, I saw an opening. We were talking about the Buddhist perspective on the difference between pain and suffering. I wondered if Eliza was unconsciously *creating* suffering to avoid experiencing the pain of having had the father she did and the brother she has. She looked at me angrily and protested that she was creating goddamn nothing.

"When you send cards, invite Jeff and his wife to dinner, and call them; when you spend time thinking about what is wrong with Jeff rather than know how hollow, painful, and frightening your childhood was, you have a feeling of agency," I explained. "It's as if there were something you could do to change the situation that is breaking your heart. It is so difficult to accept that there may never be intimacy between you and your brother. There is a difference between pain and a certain kind of suffering. You did not choose the pain caused by your father's alcoholic rages or your brother's unavailability. But you are choosing suffering by continuing to try to transform Jeff.

You cannot change the past. So far, you have not been able to change your relationship with your brother. Helplessness is extremely unpleasant to feel.

"Everybody feels pain at times," I said gently, "but there is some stuff here that you are determinedly not feeling. As long as you are working so hard to stay away from your grief and your impotence to change Jeff, you will be stuck in the suffering you are creating, longing for a relationship with your brother that for now seems impossible."

Eliza looked long and hard at the glowing candle on the table. She was quiet for several minutes. "He is like my father," she finally said. "My father used to cut me off like this, too. And those were the good times. The bad times were his rages, throwing and breaking things. Hitting Jeff or me, occasionally violently. I was terrified." She began weeping noisily.

Several more months of therapy occurred until Eliza gradually stopped creating her own suffering. She gradually learned to grieve, to allow—indeed, befriend—feelings of loss and anger, both about the possibility of a loving father and of the childhood she had never had. Jeff might never change. Nor would Eliza ever have a father who was not a cold and angry drunk.

In her wonderful book *Maybe You Should Talk to Someone*, the psychotherapist Lori Gottlieb explains how excessive emotions in the present are often clues to some unfinished business of the past. There is no redo of the past, Lori tells us. All we can do is change our relationship to our feelings about it. If we do not, when some person or situation triggers childhood pain in our adult lives, we may feel stuck. Almost all of us get triggered at times and find ourselves reacting with unusual ferocity. In feeling the pain of her father's abusiveness, Eliza began to free herself. She understood that Jeff may never become the warm, connected brother she longed for, and that loss may continue in the future. Eliza's grief about her dad, when she could finally allow her tears to flow, was clean and pure. Her suffering, her attempts to avoid her pain, were keeping her trapped. The capacity to grieve freely is a great gift.

A Spark of Impenetrable Darkness

Life renews itself continually. Each time it dips into the emptiness with new vigor.
—Tirzah Firestone, The Receiving

In the wail and moan
that precedes
the birth of a people,
precedes the splitting
of the sea,
precedes the grinding
of even one grain of wheat—a flash,
a spark
of impenetrable darkness.
A roar of breath
from the bowels
of the heavens
can almost be seen
in the vapor.

Almost.

The daughter throws back
the sheets and breathes
deeply
as she climbs
from her bed.
She lumbers
toward the room,
where her father lies dying

Chapter 1: Entering the Room

as she holds
her belly,
huge with life.

Our Planet Needs Our Love

My sister Sue and her husband, Allan, live and work in South Africa on a huge swath of conservation land they call Towerland Wilderness Center. Their teaching and consulting are inspired by a Goethean practice of deep listening to inner and outer landscapes, as well as by Rudolf Steiner's teachings about anthroposophy. Sue and Allan suggest that more depends on being awake and present than we could possibly imagine. They teach that our own stories are entwined in every shift or reversal that is manifested in the world. Committed to social and environmental change, activism, and stewardship, they bring exquisite awareness of the environment and of the social world to groups and individuals. One of their primary orientations for being present and awakening is through immersion in and reflection upon the pristine wilderness of the natural world. Their land, mountainous and vast, is home to a large range of wildlife including various antelope, porcupines, baboons, many varieties of birds, reptiles, otters, bush pigs, aardvark, many kinds of wild cats, tortoises, foxes, hares, bush pig, honey badger, and other mammals. Towerland is a water catchment and is blessed by pure, alive water in perennial rivers and streams.

Alan and I visited Towerland on one of our trips to the country of our birth. We were awestruck by the aliveness of the landscape, the sounds of life all around, the absolute commandment to pay attention to the natural world. Sue and I joke about how she is in love with the land, while my thing is people. We are both also awakened to the hidden world through each other's spiritual passions. Whenever we speak, she talks of her reverence for the earth, perhaps how the light illuminated the early morning rivers that day, the kingfisher that has just flown by her window, the baboons barking in the hills. When South Africa suffers from drought, as it often does, Sue feels this in her body. When she shares her heartbreak about climate change as the planet suffers natural disasters, she opens my eyes and heart even more to the Divine in the earth, plants, animal life, the sky.

    I asked my sister recently if she knew of *dadirri*, an Australian Aboriginal practice of inner, deep listening and quiet, tuning in with the specific aim of coming to a deeper understanding of the beauty of nature. She does and has worked with a *dadirri* practitioner. *Dadirri* recognizes the inner spirit that calls us to reflect on and contemplate the wonders of God's creation. In living a spiritual life, we learn to listen. We ask of the Beloved, "What do You want of me now, in this very moment? How can I heal our land?" Deep listening almost always requires stillness and waiting. If we pay attention to the natural world each day and listen to the Holy One speaking in the language of the land, we are inspired to treat the earth with love. If we can learn to move through our days with more consciousness and reverence for the land, we bless God—and may save the planet.

    There is unity and there is separateness, the one and the many, the Divine in myriad forms. The oneness of creation is life that is happening moment to moment in the energy that sustains—or does not sustain—growth. Alan and I have been on safari several times. In the bush, also called the *veld*, there are no judgments of good and bad—just the ongoing thrust of creation. The cheetah needs to feed her cubs. She stalks a herd of Thompson's gazelles until, close enough, she springs, overtakes, and kills a small antelope. Food for the family. While the cheetahs are eating, hyenas arrive, keeping a careful distance, awaiting their turn. Vultures circle. Several are atop tall trees, watching, waiting. When, after a long time, all have eaten and then drunk from one of the rivers, lakes, or swamps, they rest. A variety of animals, flora, and fauna exist on the same landscape. Some peaceably, others not.

It is difficult to always hold the truth that we are in heaven here and now, that how we see the world around us and what we do makes a difference. But when we take the time to reflect on life as it is being breathed, we cannot but have our attention drawn to the sacred. Everything is sacred. The bush is always burning. It simply takes awareness to see this.

Chapter 1: Entering the Room

One or Two

A theology that understands God as the eternal dialectical dance between presence and transcendence, between the revealed and the mysterious.
—Arthur Green, *Radical Judaism*

Does the droplet
of salt
water
in
the wave
in
the ocean
in
the universe
know

it is God?

I will
spend
my winter
praying
for an
answer

as my feet
dance

on

the edge

while sand,
sun and
sky
ponder
the very same
question.

Inspired by an ongoing conversation with my friend Susie K.

Chapter 1: Entering the Room

Our Own Unique Way

The very moment I awaken each morning, I pray the *Modah Ani* blessing. *Modah Ani* means "I give thanks."

> *I thank You, God,*
> *Creator of Life,*
> *Eternal One,*
> *for restoring my soul*
> *with love,*
> *filled with*
> *Your eternal trust.*

I have always loved the last two lines of this blessing. God *trusts* us. I often begin my spiritual practice of journaling soon after my morning blessings. One day I wrote to my Love:

Thanks, Beloved, for this day, this moment. You ask us to begin every day recalling our covenant with You—You'll help us heal, and if we pay attention to Your beloved planet and *know* ourselves more fully, we may help heal You in Your world. If we listen deeply to our hurt and wounded parts, we may be less likely to firehose our *shmutz* into the world—our opinions, harsh judgments, bad habits, beliefs, addictions, codependent behaviors, unhealthy patterns. If we're more awake, we can also offer our beauty more, in magical and everyday ways—like painting neighborhood cows or roosters that look eerily genuine, or making fish tacos that cause even our eight-year-old to groan in pleasure. We can volunteer at the food bank, visit elderly relatives, take several breaks from technology, pay attention to our hearts, our bodies, our brothers and sisters. *Tikkun ha-nefesh* in the service of *tikkun ha-olam*—the healing of souls in the service of the healing of the world. I know this is a forever request from You, God. Is this what You trust us to do, to listen for Your guidance on a daily, even momentary basis? And, if so, could You please speak a little louder?

Thank You, Beloved, for the dream that told me *There is the comfort of praying the prayers of those who have gone before us. But we each have to find our own unique way.*

Even now as I reflect on the dream I had so many years ago, I am moved. In Hebrew we talk of *keva* and *kavanah*. *Keva* is the stable, fixed liturgy we pray daily or in worship, like the morning blessing above. It's the prayer of community, generation upon generation, whose melody originated before our great-grandmother was born. *Kavanah* means "intention," and refers to the private, personal way we talk with the Divine. I'm more of a *kavanah* woman.

When our mother was dying, my sister Vicki and I had the idea of creating a visitors' book for family and friends. In the last several weeks of her life, our mom, Judy, who was quite the firebrand in her day, lay in a comatose, unresponsive state. When we—daughters, husbands, grandchildren, and friends—sat at her bedside, we wrote in the book. We also took pleasure in reading the often cheeky and provocative messages we were writing to one another. We knew Mom would never read the book, never know how many visitors she had. She would have loved the attention. She would have dimpled and laughed with joy. Vicki and I had fun and teased one another lovingly on a daily basis. The book made an unbearable time less painful.

One day I sat by Mom's bedside. I felt tearful as I read the loving message Vicki had written to me: "Maybe your prayers for Mom to know of your growing love for Judaism will never be answered, but I get it." I closed the small, green, leather-covered book and sighed in gratitude, in sorrow. Remarkably, some moments later, our mother, whom I had never heard speaking Hebrew, suddenly began to pray: *Yitgadal v'yitkadash sh'mei raba*. This is the first line of *Kaddish*, an ancient Jewish prayer sequence regularly recited in the synagogue service when someone has died. The prayer, which glorifies life and praises the Divine, is full of thanksgiving, despite the death about which the congregants are chanting. It concludes with a prayer for universal peace. Maybe Mom was praying for herself. Maybe she was aligning herself with the belief that life and God are glorious, although she was dying. Not much inclined to a relationship with Judaism or the Holy, she seemed to have an archetypal connection in her soul to the *Kaddish*. I know there is this connection in me.

Recondite

There once was light. Now it has been forgotten.
　　—Lawrence Kushner, River of Light

There, at the edge of the sandbar
where
the light, on this quiet gray
day
has settled, a line of white waves
stretches
like a sideways thread from heaven.
Near
the turquoise strip of ocean a lone
pelican
skims, then plunges. I stand here
bereft
with longing for someone beside
me
who might cry "Oh!"

Chapter 1: Entering the Room

Uncertainty and Unknowing

During one of the many challenging times in my life, I received a remarkable dream imperative: *I was to row alone to an island, on God's holy day, the thirteenth, and plant seeds of uncertainty and unknowing.* Little did I know that this dream, one of the most significant spiritual curricula of my life, was guiding me to what I would need to do, again and again—undertake the spiritual challenge of living with uncertainty and unknowing. "Piece of cake," I said to Alan. "I know about uncertainty and unknowing. Isn't that what the Buddhists talk about?" I imagined there would be one nice little island to row to—three hours away, at most—and one bag of seeds to plant. After that, I would be reaping fruit for the rest of my life. Happy ever after. Me and God, all enlightened. However, as I discover—to my dismay—each time I am compelled to obey the Divine, there is not one but an archipelago of islands to which I have to row.

In order to meet the Holy One most deeply, we have to keep surrendering more of what we know. I learn more, always, about surrender on psychological, spiritual, and existential levels. I tell my directees that what we think and desire counts for something. Mainly, though, the Divine is the major shareholder in our company. We need to keep pausing and listening. We need to hold our wounded selves with kindness, tenderness. We need to keep waking up to who we are, rather than who we'd like to be. We need to weep our grief and yell our anger. Life can be devastatingly unpredictable. In all this we are at the mercy of the Beloved.

If we're attuned to life's unfolding, moment by moment, we will likely experience a good dose of wonder, awe, and love at the miracle of existence. We will also know sorrow, anger, confusion, and fear about the inescapably dark side of life. In 2019 I was invited into more consciousness through a long visit with my time of dread—the worst I had ever known. Rummaging around in the dregs of my psyche was a spectacular spiritual crisis, an invitation to another layer of surrender. Is it possible that the seemingly benign catalyst of hosting a webinar kicked me into my room? I don't know. I was invited by Spiritual Directors International to create a webinar for four consecutive weeks on dreams and poetry as spiritual practices. I would be alone the first week and have guests of my choice for the subsequent three weeks. While I felt anxiety as I made my decision, I told myself that the older we get, the more life invites us to hold fear with compassion and gentleness. So, with apprehension, I said yes. I did not count on being thrown into a process that lasted for over four months and left me stripped quite bare.

There are times in my life when God has felt absent because each day seemed to be more than I could handle. This four-month period was one of them. Somehow, I managed each day well enough. I never stopped praying, even though I was beset by darkness and anxiety over which I simply had no control. The two years of crisis I endured, beginning with the time of dread, taught me more than I ever imagined possible about strengths I did not know I had.

I had a dream early in this dark period: *I meet a woman named Savage. In the dream I think "She is the enemy and I won't give her money." But there is another woman in the dream who owns a guesthouse. She insists on welcoming both of us.* The dream made me think of the poem The Guesthouse, by Jalaluddin Rumi, which tenderly invites us to accept, indeed welcome, all aspects of who we are.

I have thought countless times about this very explicit

dream. I trust my dreams as guidance, for they come from my unconscious mind, and I can't manufacture or control them. The dream points to how people and life can be both welcoming and frightening. Savage and the kind, accepting owner of the guesthouse are polarities in my psyche. I need them both. I am invited to integrate the savage, wild, uncontrollable side of life and psyche into my wholeness. There are many ways to think of Savage. She could be some deposit into my psyche when I was a young, highly sensitive, porous child. I am a Jewish woman. I have distant relatives who did not survive the Holocaust. I have dreams of the Holocaust. The dream tells me to give Savage money. In the dream world, money may represent energy and attention. I need to learn to welcome, or at least accept, the more savage aspects of my psyche, those parts of me that are not squeaky clean and nice.

Life is often savage. Hurricanes, fires, floods show no mercy. We need only to think of the multitudes felled by COVID-19. I need to see life's savagery with clear eyes and, wherever possible, combat it, and where it is not, accept it. It is often not possible to tame life.

The shadow of the psyche is simply those aspects of ourselves of which we are unconscious. We all have light and dark shadows. Confronting our darkness—pride, greed, envy, fear, alienation, judgment—is essential to wholeness. Discovering our light shadow—silliness, irreverence, wild affection, the ability to create savvy blogs that engage, amuse and teach, the insistence on play rather than perfection—is life-giving. During the time of preparing for and presenting the webinar, my resident free-floating anxiety seemed to circle and then land on my relationship with sleep. The time of dread preceded the two worst years of my life. I began to realize that I was grappling with something bigger and more frightening than anything I had ever experienced. In anguish, I sought to banish my dread, anxiety, and confusing grief, to no avail. I sought certainty from a place of desperation. There was no knowing, there was no certainty. Pema Chödrön, a Tibetan Buddhist nun, teaches that nothing ever goes away until it has taught us what we need to know. What I had to learn was that many times, I cannot know.

Savage—A Lament in Two Parts

> *It is almost humorous to discover how many names are used to point to that which is ineffable.*
> —Tirzah Firestone, The Receiving

Flame of Darkness.
Rush of Water.
Nothingness.
Who?
The Name.
Indwelling.
Flow of Divine Seed.
Compassionate One.

Seventy-two names
I'm told You have—almost
as many
as my ghastly years.
What in hell am I to call
You?

Hey You!
If You want me to remember
You, Your goddamn names,
all the rigid rules and laws—
how about Being
a little kinder
to me.

Do You remember me,

that I have cancer?
Again.
Help me, damn it,
choose life.

****

How do we manage to love God with our dark side?
—Tirzah Firestone, *The Receiving*

"Give it up, girl," You tell
me. "You think too much.
All the books, words,
structures and strictures—
stop bloody running in place."

I'm an ant, trapped
under glass, trying
to figure out
what You mean
by this stupid life.

And You?

You sit around with Satan.
Sometimes I think of Job.
Is it Savage I hear
guffawing
as You preach
about life and death
and choice?

Chapter 1: Entering the Room

Sometimes I hate
You. Then I remember
that hate,
the pundits say,
is angry love.

Beginner's Certificate

During the four months of dread, I prayed for escape from days that felt hooded and malevolent. I tossed and twisted fretfully many nights. I yearned to banish dread, confusion, profound unknowing, and feelings of impossible impotence. I told myself, sometimes kindly, sometimes impatiently, that there are times when life is beyond understanding. Maybe, as someone suggested, I was meeting God's shadow. And still, surrender felt impossible and terrifying. Like Job, for all my faithfulness to my spiritual life and the Holy One, I was lost. There is no escaping our humanity, but I began to have theories and solutions to try to control my searing vulnerability. I would take half a sleeping pill, do mindfulness meditation, practice deep breathing. I would have a session with my Jungian analyst, speak to Alan about my anguish in the morning, not speak to Alan. Alan is my "face," as I tell him. He listens with such an open mind and heart that I can listen most deeply to myself. Perhaps this is what we intuit, a love that is complete. Just reading of God's absolute love is a comfort. Perhaps we all yearn to gaze upon *this* face of the Beloved, the face of love that will forever transform our anguish.

I kept thinking, "This is it. I have the answer." But time and again, while I learned a great deal about life and myself that went into the compost heap of who I am, I did not find anything to banish my dread. Sometimes I was courageous. Sometimes I felt sorrow and compassion for myself. At other times I became annoyed and I chastised myself, full of imperatives on how my ego must simply surrender to God. *Simply.* There was no way to escape the pain of being alive, the dread of encountering something so much larger than I. Nothing worked. It seemed I needed to stay where I was.

    Pema Chödrön once received the gift of a silver necklace with a pendant in the shape of a dog tag. On it were the words *Sit. Stay. Heal.* I was being invited into new levels of suffering, to experience the absence of control. I was once more an initiate. It is by accepting the call of darkness and staying with wherever our soul leads that transformation may occur. Rather than banish my anguish, I was being called to stay with dread, with pain, with anxiety I could not control. I was being called on to have compassion for myself in my surrender to the story I was having trouble reading. I never lost trust in God's existence, and my prayers and faith did not waver. Yet I could not feel the loving presence to which I was so accustomed. In addition to turning to my six for inspiration and comfort, I tore through my wonderful library at home. All of this to no avail.

    It took more than four months of simply staying with myself in my anxious moments in the day, and beholding my tender pounding heart in the night, to love the dickens out of my blessed, messy parts. I learned, at least sometimes, to cradle myself as I was not sufficiently accepted as a sensitive, vulnerable girl. I discovered a new level of raw humanity and felt tender remorse for my hubris—all the times I believed I knew how to manage life and suffering. As I stumbled through these days, I began to be blessed with a level of compassion I did not know existed—for myself and others. The more open I was, the kinder others became. Vulnerability can be very inviting.

    After four months, the awful terror suddenly seemed to leave. Two weeks later I was diagnosed with colon cancer, and, strangely, perhaps miraculously, I was able to face the diagnosis and treatment with a modest degree of equanimity. It seemed that my suffering during the time of dread had at least somewhat burned away my illusion of having control. Were my body and soul telling me that something awful was around the bend? I don't know.

I had had breast cancer in 1988 and am considered cured. The pain of having cancer once more, enduring five weeks of radiation and chemotherapy and knowing that surgery was in my future was daunting. But God and I had found each other again and I had an odd sense of peace.

Pema Chödrön was correct: Nothing goes away until it has taught us what we need to know. I now had a beginner's certificate in surrender. I have decided on my major: to give up the belief that I am in control. I am currently working on my intermediate—for the rest of my life, I suspect.

CHAPTER 2: ENCOUNTERING MYSTERY

The Divine

Even though I cannot *know* the Divine, I believe that God is everything—the breath that creates existence, moment to moment; the great intelligence wanting to know itself through the minds and souls of humans; the source of love and light; all that is dark and frightening; and the mother of extreme noodging. The One includes humans, ants, grass blades, and even old pine tables that we know to be particles of living matter.

Why does the Divine keep creating life, revealing Godself? I suspect that life is God's ongoing experiment that has resulted in some abysmal failures but many more spectacular successes. Simply put, God is the oneness of existence, the divine spark in each of us, and in everything else, too. And God's godding, in the forever ongoing creation of the cosmos—with its stars, planets, solar systems, in the sun and the rain, and all human, animal and plant life—is, I think, primarily an experiment in love. When we argue and wrestle with the "not-love" parts, perhaps we help the Holy One awaken some more.

For me, God is an experience, and despite the less-than-charming aspects of the Holy One, I am in love with the Beloved. For more than forty years, in my desire to be conscious and present to life as it is, I have been listening to God—through my life, in my thoughts, body, emotions, and dreams.

I am in synagogue on Shabbat. The cantor begins singing the prayer *Nishmat Kol Chai* (the soul of all that lives) from our prayerbook. This translation of the prayer is by Rabbi Ed Feld, the primary editor of our congregations' beautiful prayerbook which is called *Lev Shalem* which means a whole heart. The cantor sings from the Hebrew while I read the English

> *Were our mouths to fill with song as the sea*
> *our tongues to sing endlessly like countless waves,*
> *our lips to offer limitless praise like the sky,*
> *our eyes to shine like the sun and the moon,*
> *our arms to spread heavenward like eagle's wings,*
> *and our feet as swift as deer,*
> *we would still be unable to fully express our gratitude to You,*
> *Adonai (my Lord) our God and God of our ancestors,*
> *or to praise Your name for even one of the myriad moments*
> *of kindness with which You have blessed our ancestors and us.*

My God-tears arrive and I think "that's about right."

A Different Lens

My friend Bev, a psychotherapist, reminisces about a period in her life some years ago when, in minor crisis, she had sought the support and insight provided by a mature psychotherapy group. I comment on how smart she was to seek a compassionate environment where she could listen deeply to others and to herself. Bev muses as we walk: "I received a great deal from the group. I am in a good place now, so I don't need it anymore. But I miss the way I used to feel after each session." Her voice becomes quieter. "I would say I was humanized more deeply. During and after sessions, I saw people and the world through a different lens. I seem to have somewhat misplaced that lens." My friend is a person of substance and was one before the group, so she is not talking about becoming more decent. Bev is reflecting on seeing the world more spiritually, on paying deepest attention. She is expressing awe and reverence for people's beauty, for their vulnerability and humanity. She speaks of her wonder about a heightened consciousness of life's darkness and its light. Bev is talking about being awake. It can be difficult to sustain this kind of perspective on our own. Community is a priceless container for kindness. I tell Bev a little about spiritual direction groups, and she says, "Hmm, interesting..." in that way people do when they have no intention of doing what you may be hinting at.

    A regular spiritual practice can help us sustain our lens of compassion for ourselves and the world. A spiritual practice can be anything we do regularly with the intention of being more present, more awake. One of my directees is an avid cyclist who uses her time of riding to be present and quiet, to listen to her mind, she says. I ask what she does in the winter when outdoor riding is impossible. "I seldom miss a day," she tells, "but if the weather is too icy or snowy, I ride on my stationary bike and let my thoughts come. Or not."

En Route

For a word to truly contain God, says the mystic, it must at once embrace...both endless answers and eternal questions.
—Arthur Green, *Judaism for the World*

We fly
above generous white clouds,
pillows of the possible—
a world
where serpents
of darkness
have no place.

I use
some of the time
to answer
the *End of Life*
questions
our lawyer
has asked us to complete.
Questions that cause me
to scratch my head.

Which of these do you fear most
as you near the end of your life:

- Loss of mobility
- Loss of mental capacity
- Incontinence
- Pain

- *Confusion*
- *Loneliness*

How can I *know*?
Would I opt
for chemotherapy
if taken down
by another cancer?
Might I agree
to yet another blood
transfusion to prolong
a tattered life?

The serpent,
as the story goes,
seduced Adam and Eve
from perfection.
Awakened them
to a life
of not knowing.

All I can think of
as I read the questions,
is how I cried
when we said goodbye
to our family. Fifteen
grands, nine great-grands
and their parents,
in the holy city,
Jerusalem. How

The Light of God's Shadow

I had to peel sweet
Rivky from my body.

Until this visit
she barely spoke to us,
her English shy,
tucked well below
Yiddish and Hebrew.

Soft pillows of cloud
have given way
to jagged streaks of black,
shot through
with white and gold.

"Life is larger
than we are,"
my daughter-in-law
had said, hugging me
fiercely.

Somewhere
in the back
of my mind
a slither of green
streaks into the undergrowth
and disappears.

The above poem was inspired by a dream in which *my daughter-in-law Ilana tells me there is a small snake in a large salad. I don't want to look at it, but she insists.*

Humility

The challenge of theology is both prayer and hope...and to speak thoughtfully and with intention.
—Michael Fishbane, Fragile Finitude

If we but knew
all
that shapes
our encounter
with the other—

our narratives, mythologies, stories,
blood pressure,
heritage three generations
back—

even

the relation
at this very moment
of the moon
to the earth—

we would
before uttering
one
unkind
word

lash

ourselves
to the mast.

Chapter 2: Encountering Mystery

Anxiety-Squared: One Origin of My Suffering—Maybe

My father's death after his second heart attack thrust me into waking up. I was thirty-three at the time. My four-year training to become a gestalt therapist began right after my father's death and was followed six years later by my immersion in Jungian psychology. My first Jungian analyst, Fraser Boa, told me that one day I would be grateful for my wounds. I thought he was mad. But gradually I came to understand his wisdom. Although never grateful for pain and suffering, I have learned that my wounds—together with my genetic makeup, my sensitive psyche, and the circumstances of my life—drew me to seek connection with my soul, with God. That began then and still occurs now. My father, an anxious and vulnerable man, wanted so much to be different. During our childhood, my two sisters and I loved him fiercely. I only realized as an adult that he was pretending he was as robust and carefree as he wished to be. And as much as he wanted to be free of *his* anxiety and sadness, my father could not bear it if I, his oldest child, was in distress. I learned from an early age that my unhappiness meant that something was very wrong. Anxiety was an impending catastrophe. With great tenderness and every intention of kindness, my father led me away from life's ordinary fears and sorrows. I remember telling him I was scared because I would be going to high school after the summer holidays. "Mind over matter," my father said kindly. "Focus on the positive." What was needed was some version of "Tell me more. It's okay to be scared. Let's touch and hold it together." I still love my father fiercely, and know that he was always doing the best he could.

To compound matters, my vulnerability and sensitivity were nuisances to my practical and impatient mother. Mine was a common story. There was no place in my childhood for all of me. I learned that the messy, fearful, less contained aspects of my psyche needed to be packed away, chaotic feelings banished. This is the origin of my greatest suffering—I became anxious and distressed when anxious or distressed. This spiral of *tzuris*, as we call trouble in Yiddish, was far worse than any pain I might have felt for the woes of an ordinary life.

In the dark times during 2019 and 2020, in times of struggle and pain, my carefully tended psychospiritual garden offered no respite or wisdom. "First-world problem," you might have said. "Do more therapy. Surrender to God." But despite years and years of psychotherapy, Jungian analysis, and spiritual direction; despite conversations with Alan, my beloved sisters, wise and psychologically intuitive friends; despite pulling out all the stops in my praying to God, I was still captive, at times, to what I came to call "anxiety-squared"—anxiety about sadness, anxiety about anxiety. God's face was concealed from me.

I have spent much of my life working with these howling animal parts—within myself and the people who have blessed me with their trust to be their psychotherapist and spiritual companion. I am tender and compassionate with others when they are sad or anxious. During this time in my life, though, I often could not find compassion for myself. I reacted with a second layer of distress when I was distressed, and became caught in a spiral of struggle and rumination. Over my lifetime I have learned how important it is for us to keep working on ourselves, awakening to who we are rather than who we wish to be. Questions of discernment may never be as important as when the call to awaken, through anguish, arrives. When we know ourselves more, we are less constrained and contaminated by our "stuff," and can listen more openheartedly to ourselves and others. This process of deep, attuned listening is holy, and it begins with our own psychospiritual work.

Going in and down, feeling the pain, staying with ourselves with soft bellies and open hearts, both redeems us and brings us closer to the Holy One. In the time of COVID-19, some are saying, "Focus on the positive" or "Get over it. This is your life now." "Getting over stuff" does not work for me. I trust that grief is sacred and needs witness. Allowing pain to run its course is holy work. Existence is a process of cocreation with the Holy One, so when I stay with my suffering, when I keep praying to God from my broken heart, the Divine often feels closer to me. In heaven, it is said, the gates of tears are the only gates that are never locked. The fear anyone experiences when encountering the dark side of mystery is mythic. Staying present to the unknowable may ultimately yield the beauty and wonder of being intensely alive. Into the dark side of the One we go, and there, in God's timing, we may meet the light.

Nobody Holds All the Aces

For Jung, as for the Kabbalists...there cannot be a single valid interpretation of a dream.
—Sanford Drob, Kabbalistic Visions: C. G. Jung and Jewish Mysticism

I am climbing some stairs,
writing a poem. God
is playing poker. Dark
blue nail polish. Strong,
capable hands. God
points to me—"This
one is lovely."

I flush.

Then God says

"There is nothing
big enough to fill the hole."

Chapter 2: Encountering Mystery

One Eye

Readers are invited (to embark on a journey within the words)
as necessary partners in the journey of decoding.
—Melila Hellner-Eshed, A River Flows from Eden

Honeycomb.
Layer upon layer,
lattice of cells.

Tiny hexagon
upon tiny
hexagon.

Perfect geometry.

Windows
into existence.

How do bees
know
such architecture?

I am writing
a letter
to God—

One eye

seeing
the one

eye
of God
seeing me.

Dear Companion,
please
help me
decode
my dream.

Maybe Not?

Imagine a cartoon sequence showing a woman and a man trudging up the proverbial mountain. At the top, the guru. The man begs for instructions on the meaning of life. The guru, all wise demeanor and closed eyes, intones, "Life is like a river."

"What! #!" The seeker is furious and begins choking the guru. The loin-clothed, cross-legged wise man shrugs and says, "Or maybe not?"

This cartoon—part Buddhist commentary, part Catskill shtick—offers guidance about the meaning of life and the Divine. How can we know anything with certainty? The only God we understand can't be God. Nonetheless, as long as I can remember, I have been chasing Mystery trying to find the source of my joy and anguish. My poems of gratitude and lament are love stories and anguished cries to the One I keep seeking and finding and losing. They help me unearth some words to speak of the ineffable, for whom no words will do. I might as well, though, write my theories about the meaning of life on toilet paper, as a dream once bade me. Like the man and woman at the top of the mountain, I seek enlightenment. Good luck. Yet all the reading, writing, scribbling, scrubbing, musing, and weeping in joy and lament help me wake up some more.

The guru is also correct. As it is seen in the Zohar, we are always being given life by the river that eternally flows from Eden, being nourished by the crystalline drops of dew that trickle eternally from the One who loves—every single moment of life. For as long as forever, the Source of Life has been and is doing creation. Evolution—in every single form of life—is now. Think about it: At this very moment, as you read these words—sitting, standing, lying down; wearing your ratty old sweats or those new jeans you bought before the pandemic—every breath you receive is a gift. You are being breathed. The Source of Life creates delphiniums and Dobermans, carrots and COVID-19, and your very own dear self. The river of life never stops flowing, and no matter what your story, the sun will rise every single blessed day. And somewhere in the world, a baby Doberman, just born, will curl against her mother, and elsewhere carrottops will peek from the earth. And when the force of life no longer flows, say, into a body ravaged with cancer (a quick prayer of thanks that I am still around) and that person is gone, the sun will still rise. The *miracle* of it...Think about it.

Mandela

Only when we know what lies within us can we know what lies beyond us.
—Tirzah Firestone, *The Receiving*

Chocolate cake, a ripe, creamy Brie.
Your granddaughter's first tooth
in a mouth full of gums. Hush

of the concert hall before Bach's
double concerto vibrates
your body. Light streaks
surreal after a clap
of thunder. Earth's

loamy smell during
the wild storm. Your
beloved who wanders
in, seeking his glasses
for the fourth time

that day. The great white
heron almost hidden
in the curlicued mangroves.
Comfort of the old
gray chair, your feet up
on the footstool.

Loving
this kind of life

The Light of God's Shadow

    is easy.

           How did you
           do it, Madiba,
           in your eight
               by eight cell?

The Way Out Is Through

In her spiritual direction sessions, Myra gradually learns to accept the current darkness of her psyche. In the early days of our sitting together, she describes herself as someone for whom the Holy One is mainly love and light. But after being fired unexpectedly from her position as a hospital administrator, Myra feels fear, anger, and confusion far greater than any distress she has previously known. She asks me to help her feel "like herself," to escape a darkness that feels oppressive, engulfing, terrifying. "The demons seem to have arrived," she reports. Myra is not happy when I suggest that our blessed work is to descend into this very place from which she is running. This is "herself," too. I tell her I will hold the space with her when we sit together and pray for her during and after sessions.

Myra trusts the God work, and over a period of several months she allows herself to sit in the darkness—sometimes quietly, sometimes weeping, sometimes even raging. Her dreams become quite pointed, and she has several of teeth, newborns and dealing with death. When we sit quietly and invite the dream images to amplify, she wonders if a part of her is dying— the part that, like me, had the familial injunction to always be positive and cheerful, never anxious. I tell her parts never die. We can just become more aware of them, more compassionate toward them, and better able to stop them from seizing the wheel of the bus. She begins to be hopeful that something is being born in her psyche, that new neural pathways may be developing in her brain. She asks about teeth in dreams, and I suggest that they can mean chewing, digesting, taking in new material, integrating, assimilating. They can also mean assertion, aggression, rage. Much more important, though, I tell her, are the associations the dreamer makes to images or stories. Myra thinks of her mother's dentures, of her determinedly positive behavior. She speaks of her mother's frequent directive, "Let it go," when Myra is in distress. I tell her I am not so crazy about "Let it go." There *are* times when it is healthy to become busy and engaged with life in order to manage pain. However, if we try to let go of the depth of our despair or anguish and focus on the positive too often, we may be doing a spiritual bypass. When we do deep work, we can trust the process, or God, or whatever we call deepest soul wisdom, to lift us out of despair when the mourning is done.

One day Myra reports a dream about her grandmother who had barely escaped murder in the Holocaust. Myra and I wonder whether some of the darkness she has been feeling is bigger than her own story. Our psyches often carry energy, memories, intense emotions from our ancestors. Epigenetic and family constellation therapists help us learn about a "field" that is present in several generations. In family constellation therapy, we learn that nothing or no one is to be excluded. Everything belongs in the field.

The stories of our parents and their parents have a history in our bodies, in our souls. We inherit their green eyes, their smarts, their proclivity to solitude and laughter. Our son Glen tells me, "I got my introversion from you." We also sometimes inherit their wounds. He also says, "My sensitivity, too. For the good and bad of it." If we accept the awesome reality of trauma that needs tending, and take on the courageous task of accepting the grief, rage, or terror within us, we can bless the family field by offering some healing. Sometimes it is the most sensitive member of the family who feels the intergenerational pain. After almost fifteen months, Myra's spirit and energy begin to return. She has learned that darkness is a part of her that needs compassionate and tender integration.

In my own ongoing awakening, I have learned to understand that while I can often understand more about myself and my messy places through exploring the stories of my ancestors, there are vestiges of family history I may never know. Sometimes I need to rest in unknowing. If I am able to, this may allow me to live with more freedom.

Turning toward our own darkness is one way we can offer healing to the collective. By befriending our wounds as well as our own *shmutz*—the messy ways we sometimes feel and behave—we are less likely to act out our *shmutz* on others.

The Thing Itself

The mystery of life, which is far beyond human understanding, needs a physical vehicle to carry it.
—Tirzah Firestone, The Receiving

If you stand still
for a long, long time—
look
with smoky
eyes,
breathe in,
      then out,

you may see
    movement
        just below
the surface.

Triangular fin
   slow motion, wave-like curls
break
   the water—
in
    then
out.

You might find
yourself

intoning

an almost silent
prayer.

Stand still
even longer,

you might even find
yourself

thinking

of an early story,
of how—
upon
the face
of the waters—

there was movement
and a brilliant
light.

You might even see
the thing itself—

like Michelangelo
   gazing on the block
of marble

  seeing
David
  for the first time.

Grace

It is an illusion for us to believe that we have a complete or even "true" view of God.
—Sanford Drob, Kabbalah, Jungian Psychology, and the Challenge of Contemporary Atheism

You look different, Grace,
from how I usually see you
behind the counter—
your red uniform,
name tag.
You seem radiant here
as we pass on Bathurst Street.
Almost noble.
The nose-ring you *don't* wear
when you're bagging groceries
catches the sun.
Your gel-studded spiky hair.
Boots black. Jeans tight.
Is this your girlfriend?
She smiles and nods
as you talk and talk and talk.

I nod at you
but you don't see me.
I'm of that age where I blend
into the surroundings—Dollar Store
on the corner. Shoppers Drug
Mart. In line
for coffee

at Second Cup.

I know you're God, Grace.
If you knew
I am,
would you also
get goose bumps as we pass—
me, on my daily, old lady
walk. You, with your wild,
defiant beauty. And your girlfriend,
smiling and nodding
at God.

Grace, Again

I have one of my "moments" as I walk down the stairs on my way to prepare lunch. It is early spring, a gray day. I had my first COVID-19 vaccine yesterday and I am tired, a bit fuzzy-headed. There is no apparent cause for this sudden moment of intense presence—indeed, it is counterintuitive, a pure gift. I reflect on all that might have made me feel this awake, alive, joyful. But despite much in my life that I am currently grateful for, I cannot draw a cause-effect conclusion, nor can I make moments like these happen. Sheer blessing, they are strung like pearls on the long necklace of my life, and when they occur, I am arrested by gratitude. I tell Alan about my moment as I take the soup from the fridge, and I touch my face in wonder. The traces of awakening feel like the breath of the Divine against my skin—my cheek, my neck, the back of my hand. I whisper, "Thank You."

Charlie and Chatty Cathy

Alan and I sit in the living room for our biweekly "Shabbat spiritual session." When we meet like this, the quality of our listening and talking is different than in the daily and frequently lengthy conversations we have. It is my turn to go first. Sometimes I arrive with an agenda, but today is different. I shut my eyes for a few moments. The stillness is luscious. The feeling is of going in and down—head to heart—to listen for what wants to be said, almost like free association. I feel strangely empty yet embodied, utterly received by Alan and by the deepest place in me I call God. I listen for several moments, then I do my best to give voice to words that seem to issue from a place that is neither just mind nor body, but both. Mystery is whispering. The very air shimmers and the moment brims with life. Despite the fact that there is currently much darkness in the world, I am inspired and nourished by the thoughts, questions, and emotions that arrive.

Some say these days of lockdown are boring, monotonous. Not for me. My inner life, when I access it—in solitude, reading, writing, walking, and in deepest connection—frequently teems with wonder. I tell Alan it is like this with prayer. You can say, "I sure hope so-and-so gets better," or you can shut your eyes and hope becomes prayer.

When my friend Ruth and I were in our early thirties, we went through a process of discovering many different ways of expanding consciousness. We talked excitedly of the works of Pyotr Ouspensky, George Gurdjieff, Colin Wilson, the LSD experimenters Baba Ram Dass and Timothy Leary, Fritz Perls, Ken Wilbur, Sigmund Freud, Carl Jung, and others. We were cocky—sure we had discovered something entirely original. One day Ruth and I, high on being present and our love for each other, fell into a long silence. "What do we call all this?" I asked after some time. "Charlie," Ruth shot back instantly.

There are countless ways to awaken to the reality of life, to the miracle of noticing the always burning bush. Even when the fire is too close for comfort and I experience pain—because of COVID-19, my cancer, and Eli's death—being awake is desirable.

Ruth and I once called presence, consciousness, and love "Charlie." I now call it God. Ruth practices Dzogchen Buddhism. I discovered Kabbalah around the time Ruth discovered Dzogchen, and I have been a passionate beginner ever since. It's the Divine all the way for me, despite the somewhat erratic nature of the Holy One.

I companion Jodi in spiritual direction. She is a gifted writer and visual artist, and she has a wild and funny imagination. In a recent session, she grumbles about the Divine. "I used to test God when I was a girl," she confesses. I would say, "If you exist, God, make my Chatty Cathy doll fall from the shelf." We roar. Later in the session, Jodi speaks of feeling a bit defeated by life, by all the tasks required to manage her home and work life. Her days feel challenging. Not temperamentally tidy and organized, she sometimes feels overwhelmed with housekeeping. "What do I do?" she asks. "How do I connect with God and get direction?" I remind her of the blessed question: "What now, my Love?" I say that we may "get" nothing, but listening itself is good. Jodi and I shut our eyes. After a few minutes she peeks at me. "I heard I need to start small. I get daunted so easily. So, here goes: God, please help me put the cutlery away and wipe down the counter. Amen." She looks embarrassed, as if being foolish or, even worse, spiritually recalcitrant. I have tears in my eyes. She is listening.

The Palace of Understanding

The seed of Wisdom requires a palace of Understanding in order to develop.
—Melila Hellner-Eshed, Seekers of the Face

It begins with one seed—
planted deep, humus moist,
just enough sun, rain,
days, nights
of deepest consolation

till the new begins
to tremble forth—
one green shoot
breaking into life.

There is no way
to hurry this.
Rest a while,
pray for understanding.

In the meantime
feel the Breath—
air against your cheeks,
back of your neck,
enfolding your naked hand.

CHAPTER 3: DOING THE WORK

Anne Frank and the Miracle of Reading and Writing

"I hope I will be able to confide everything to you, as I have never been able to before, and I hope you will be a great comfort and support to me," wrote Anne Frank at the beginning of her diary. I was ten when I read those words. Anne's prolific writing took place while she was in hiding with her family for two years, during the Nazi occupation of the Netherlands. The family was apprehended in 1944 and Anne died of typhus in Bergen-Belsen in 1945. She called her journal "Kitty." I call mine God.

In her dazzling book *Forest Dark*, Nicole Krauss says, "Writing had begun so differently for me. At the age of fourteen or fifteen, I'd grasped at it as a way to organize myself—not just to explore and discover, but to consciously grow myself."

I have been under the spell of the magic of language since I was a girl. Reading and writing are two of my keys to awakening—two primary spiritual practices in which I talk to and listen for the Beloved. I always have several books on my night table—my spiritual teachers and also fiction. I love good stories, and besides, everything is a potential teacher. Reading is inspirational, provocative, and nourishing—balm that heals. I immerse myself in words and language every day, along with my morning coffee—when the world of dreams still enfolds me. Then I write. The reading and writing become almost simultaneous, entwined like the symbol of infinity. It is hard to know where one begins and the other ends.

Writing helps me listen to my soul—to that which has

brought me joy, and to the confusion, pain, uncertainty that may plague me. My early morning writing is a form of one-on-one sessions with the Great Listener, sometimes a kind of sweeping through of the day or days before. I write from the inside out, which turns life into prayer. I write my reverence—of moments that stopped me in wonder. I write of gratitude for those I love. I write my lament, my confusion, asking for help from the One. I record my dreams for guidance. I write poetry and prose. In this process I discover something quite wondrous. After my reflective writing seems to be coming to a natural end, I pause and then address God directly. "Beloved," I write, or maybe "Holy One." As soon as I write directly to the Beloved, my God tears arrive, and I feel more deeply connected to the Divine. I am forever in awe of the generative and transformational aspects of writing, of how by writing deeply and nakedly from within our lives, old patterns of a lifetime may gently transform.

One of my poetry mentors, Cathy Smith Bowers, shares her own process of writing poetry. She receives a numinous image through a dream, a memory. Perhaps she sees a person, something in church, a trash can that is suddenly compelling. She knows she must write. "Write into the abiding image," she advises. "Write into the abiding image. And then keep doing that until the image tells you what you need to know."

"The book," I keep telling Alan, "is writing me, helping me wake up. I have no choice but to write."

I write not to teach but to learn. Life has become more wondrous, more alive because of my engagement with the book. Countless times I say, "*This* is what it's all about. I must remember to say *this*." I read and write to be stretched between the polarities of what I know and what I don't—mainly what I don't.

Writing poetry is of a different order than my "Dear Diary" to the Beloved. Edward Hirsch wrote, "A poem is a hand, a hook, a prayer." The work of my six frequently constellates a poem. Their words caress or poke at my mind, my heart, and then images and emotions arise that spin me around. All I need to do is step out of the way of my speeding hand. Poems demand a listening heart. Once the poem is written, and I have read it aloud, I understand why I had to come to a dead stop, listen, begin writing. I am usually writing to or about God. Mostly the poems are what I affectionately call *drek*, which is Yiddish for "trash." But that's okay. Writing, like life, is work in progress. I usually know immediately when a poem is a keeper, but I don't try to write keepers. I write to hear what my soul is telling me.

The Words to Say It

Y-H-W-H speaks to us in thunderclaps; it takes a Moses to translate God's thunder into words.
—Arthur Green, Seek My Face

There are none
yet
the imperative
to try
is ceaseless.

Instead, a field—
several acres choked
with weeds
twisted
tree branches
old orange crates
newspapers dating
back several years
broken bottles, rusted
tin cans
even an old brown velvet waistcoat
buttons intact.

You have spent your life
clearing your corner.
Your hands
are rough
your eyes tired.
Your body is strong.

You are grateful.

You sit.

Your eyes prickle
with strange tears
as you ache
with longing
to say what you—
no Moses—
cannot.

The air is warm and moist
on your skin.

The Biggest Adventure, or What Now, My Love?

When I was a practicing psychotherapist, I had a client who spoke often of her work as a spiritual director. Allie's relationship with God, and her passion for the guiding spirit within, transfixed me. I was also beginning to treasure the more frequent spontaneous silences occurring in most of the psychotherapy sessions. The silences seemed to arise from reverence or anguish. Allie told me of the book *Jewish Spiritual Guidance*, by Kerry Olitzky and Carol Ochs. I instantly ordered it, devoured the teachings, and knew immediately that I wanted to become a spiritual director. There were no training programs for aspiring Jewish spiritual directors yet, so I went from Toronto to New York to meet with Carol. We had a long-ranging and wonderful conversation. Oddly, what I remember most is what Carol said about Lance Armstrong, for it was a perfect framing for what has become a significant spiritual practice. The Tour de France had been completed a few days before Carol and I met, and Lance Armstrong had just had his first win. "Lance Armstrong," said Carol, "is on top of the world right now. I don't know how long he will stay there. But I feel this way every day of my life. For I am always on the biggest adventure." Carol was referring to living an intentional, spiritual life.

In 1999 Lance Armstrong had just won the Tour de France for the first time. It was a remarkable accomplishment, given that there had been some doubt at the time that he would even survive the testicular cancer he had been diagnosed with just three years earlier. Armstrong went on to win six more Tour de France titles. Many of us may know the dramatic story that subsequently unfolded—doping allegations against Armstrong that he vehemently denied, how he bribed many, sued others,

Chapter 3: Doing the Work

and tried to destroy some in his decade-long reign, always proclaiming his innocence. At the time of our meeting, neither Carol nor I had any idea of Lance Armstrong's darkness. If we did, we probably would have clucked about his badness and known, too—since we were both oriented to the both/and perspective on psyche—of his goodness. Armstrong raised and donated huge amounts of money for cancer research. Instead, we talked about being on the biggest adventure, no matter what occurred. I was a goner, and I thank Carol for the framing. Regardless of whether the moment holds terror or wonder, I check in frequently with the Holy One to see how I am to proceed. "What now, my Love? What should we do here?"

What is happening in the world around me and in my body are reality. My feeling of connection to God—or not—is the underpinning of how I navigate life. It's an inside job, after all. When I feel connected to the Divine, it is easier to be aware of and rejoice in each blessed breath I am given, to mostly make choices for the good. I wish I could report that this was my default position, but I have had countless lessons to teach me that this is not possible. Although I always know that I am on the biggest adventure, there are innumerable times when I pray to the Beloved with some version of "What the hell is going on here? Please help me learn what I need to, so I can wake up." Daily life can be daunting. Many of us have felt dread and anguish living through a prolonged and deadly pandemic, with systemic racism, in a political climate that is too frequently mean. Ideally, we make room for all our thoughts and emotions to be held with kindness, by ourselves and hopefully a loving someone else. Then we can ask, "What now? Help me move forward in a way that serves my wholeness. And also serves others."

I am happy to report that reasonably soon after meeting

Carol, I enrolled in the first-ever training program for Jewish spiritual direction offered in North America. It was called *Lev Shomea* (Listening Heart). This was 2001, and I was part of a very large group of others hungry to become spiritual directors. Becoming a spiritual director has shaped my life in countless wonderful ways. Being a psychotherapist was no longer quite enough for my soul that needed the larger container of belonging to a community of others who were devoted to a life of waking up, listening for the mystery, and being of service.

Ein-sof*

Something calls and must be heeded.
—Michael Fishbane, *Fragile Finitude*

I am rowing alone
to an island.
It is the thirteenth—
God's holy day.
The sun blazes
with ferocity.
I have been called
to plant seeds—
of uncertainty
and unknowing.

The water is calm.
Layers of blue
and navy
mirror the sky.
There is no
one, no thing,
no sound, save
the call of a loon.

I want to turn back
toward land,
green and dense
with sounds
of people and life,
loving, working,

fighting.

But I have been called
to row alone,
to this island.
From a distance
it looks like desert.
It is the thirteenth,
God's holy day.

The sun blazes
with ferocity.
I am alone.

The seeds
of uncertainty
and unknowing
jostle, impatient,
in a small,
plastic bag,
in the right
back pocket
of my blue
jeans.

I cannot remember
how they got there.

*Ein-sof: Absolute/Infinite. The God of everything and nothing.

A Vagabond in Love

Mystical writing...ensues from an ecstatic state.
   —Sanford Drob, Kabbalistic Visions

Guilty as charged,
my Lord.
I can't help it. I swear.
My intentions
are pure. I open
the creaking book.
Polish my glasses.
Make a cup of tea.

Real garden mint.

Intend to spend
hours with one
single word.

Before I know it,
a whole story
is written on virgin
paper, about
a princess who believes
she can fly
from danger
and the seduction
of perfidy.

My mind is pure

but my heart
has a mind
of its own.
No scholar, I,
just a vagabond
in love
with pictures
and castles
in the air.

Forgive me,
my Lord,
I can't help it.
I swear.

The black fire*
of the text
seems to disappear
my Lord,

in a blaze,
of white.

A midrash teaches that the primordial Torah was written with black fire on white fire, in the presence of God.

Chapter 3: Doing the Work

Meet Chip Henderson

"Give the animus something to do," my analyst told me, "or he makes a nuisance of himself." Bob didn't know he was repeating almost verbatim what a dream had told me many years before: *You have a rather nuisancey animus and a whole host of other characters in your psyche. You're going to have to learn to live with them.* I intuited my negative animus for years before he introduced himself to me in a dream. "I'm Chip Henderson," he said. Chip Henderson? Good grief! I reeled in the dream. The name conjures up images of yacht clubs and ascots, cuff links and starched shirts, dark blazers and white handkerchiefs tucked just so in the upper left-hand pocket. Not the inner figure you would imagine for a "nice Jewish girl." Control is Chip's middle name. He is opinionated, judgmental, sometimes intolerant of others, and often mean about me. Chip can turn up his nose at someone's supposed lack of psychological sophistication, inner life, or table manners. He is a know-it-all, and he believes that he has the last word on politics, religion, sex, money, child-rearing, and most of the large and tiny factors that make up a life. He's especially snooty about waking up. At times he can be dark and gloomy about my life, predicting all manner of dire eventualities, like a third cancer, or a stroke when I feel fuzzy headed for a moment. Chip is scornful about my writing, my neuroses, my lack of consciousness. He is superb at doing a double whammy on me, sending me into a complex about being in a complex. He can shame me for my "messy" reactions, disapprove of my vulnerability, point out my inability to stay conscious at all times: "After all the years of work you've done," he scoffs, in a British accent. Compared to real problems in the world, my problems and complexes are what Fritz Perls, the founder of Gestalt therapy, called "chickenshit." Nonetheless, when complexes arrive, they generally tie up energy and make us decidedly miserable. Some Jungian analysts believe that when we know our complexes and can send them packing, we have a cure.

Musings, stories, and poems come from the unconscious, from the same place as dreams—as I see it. Our dreams point to our shadow, the ways the complexes are in disguise on a particular day. Working regularly with our dreams is a way to become on first-name terms with our complexes, as the Jungians name the splinter psyches that show up in our daily lives. Dreams are other, not created by our conscious minds. All dreams are gifts, I believe, and offer wholeness and healing. Perhaps especially the darkest ones.

Complexes can be positive or negative, and they are always associated with an excessive amount of emotion. They are usually created through the small or large traumas we experienced growing up. The animus represents a woman's experience with men and the latent masculine principle within herself. On the positive side, the animus can confer courage, strength, direction, the capacity to buckle down and do the hard work. My positive animus helps me walk in subzero temperatures, do the plank in my daily exercises, and learn how to manage technology to a modest degree. He has also kept me working with my book, when sometimes I wanted to run for the hills. Chip H. is my negative animus. I like to think I have outed him and that he has lost some of his edge. Work in progress. A man with a positive anima may be sensitive, empathic, spontaneously nurturing. A man's negative anima, connected with moods and emotions, can hear criticism even when all you intended was an invitation to share in meal planning.

Einstein taught that the mind that creates the problem cannot solve it. Our problem solver lies in our unconscious. Having access to this deepest wisdom through dreams can transform our lives. We can't see our own back. Our blind spots are our blind spots.

A Poem about Boundaries

A person can be fully present, lose all awareness of self, and yet miraculously not be consumed by the "flame" of God's presence.
—Lawrence Kushner, God was in this Place, & I, i, did not know

The one who writes
watches the pen chase
the word
across the page—
with a terrible
longing
to see
what will be written
next—

This same one
stops
for a moment,
to watch
whitecaps
fence with one another
across ocean's
upturned belly,
then smiles
at the grumpy wind
chasing
and howling
at birds.

The boundaries,
you see,
are not
real,
though pen, letters,
birds, wind
and ocean
are.

First There Is a Mountain

Everything can be itself and something else.
—Sanford Drob, *Kabbalistic Visions*

Not in white, not in black,
not in red, not in green,
in no color at all
I want to write of *Shekhinah*

of the rainbow offering
garments to Moses,
as he ascends the mountain.

I want to measure the distance
from one end of the earth
to the other, glimpse light
in wild strawberries
and wilder boys.

I want to discover the river
flowing from Eden
sit on the back of the donkey,
beside the old man.

I want to find
the girl who sings

without vowels.

But you—you want me

to bear witness
as stories of lions
and donkey-drivers appear.

I refuse. You win.
First there is a mountain.
Then there is no mountain.
Then there is.

T'shuvah (Repair) and *Shmutz* Cleaning

I walk home after dropping my car off for service. I'm doing my Annie Dillard impression as I smile at the yawning and stretching of spring's sweet appearance. Trees, blossoms, and grass awaken each year, faithful to creation. I am in the ecstasy department with God. Then I remember the very difficult conversation I had with a friend yesterday. With my encouragement, Rosie had told me how inconsiderate I had been during a recent difficult period of her life. I had listened carefully, and then thanked Rosie for her feedback. Now I feel sorrow. For Rosie. For my unconsciousness. I fall in love with God once more. Another opportunity to wake up. Apologies are not sufficient, though, and I need to reflect on how my juice for my own projects can make me insufficiently thoughtful. Rosie's honesty gives me a chance to do *t'shuvah*, "repentance." I will make a date for a long walk with her soon, and will prepare her favorite all-the-veggies-in-the-world soup. Loving God is not all trees, spring blossoms, and green grass. The more we clean our *shmutz*, the more conscious we become. This helps us empty ourselves of our "stuff," and become better able to listen deeply to another.

Psyches sometimes operate in somewhat primitive, child-like ways. "Thank You, my God, for loving me. I so wanted a good parking space. Right in front of the bakery. May there be fresh chocolate almond croissants today. Can You please love me tonight by helping me sleep well?" Part of maturing spiritually may involve the ongoing realization that the Divine does not show love by making life easy. On the other hand, prayer is energy, and there is nothing wrong with praying for parking spaces, croissants and good sleeps or praying thank you. Mysticism welcomes ambiguity.

There are countless ways to do *t'shuvah*, but here I address only one—what I call *shmutz* cleaning. *Shmutz* is the mess we make when we are unconscious, act out, mess up in our lives because of the ways in which we were messed up as kids. Since life is a spiritual practice, I am particularly attentive to the times and places in my days and nights where I feel unaligned. *Shmutz* cleaning is an incomparable consciousness raiser. When I behave in unkind ways, to others or myself, when I feel excessively stirred, anxious, or disgruntled, the Holy One is surely trying to get my attention, to help me wake up to the fact that some wound or conflict has been triggered. "If it's hysterical, it's historical," someone once told me. Any time, too, I am obsessed with somebody or something, there is a call to become conscious of what is going on "underneath."

Jung said his inner life was more real to him than his outer life. I, too, am intensely introverted, but, of necessity, whenever we visit our huge family in Israel, I live primarily in outer life, in extroverted energy. My reflective writing, which includes a daily *shmutz* cleaning practice, takes a back seat. It is not that I lose my connection with the Holy One. My felt sense of the Divine is still present—tears of "yes" that arise as our grandson of seven makes the full Shabbat blessing, joy as I watch Ilana put several challah loaves in the oven. But when I don't have sufficient time for my spiritual practice of *shmutz* cleaning, the thread of connection feels more tenuous.

It always takes a while for me to find my way back to the right balance of introversion, and the route there usually involves ferreting out the latest bit of unconsciousness that has clogged up the system. This time in Israel, despite knowing better, I had tried to do the impossible—spend quality time with almost every single one of our huge brood. Little wonder I felt off-balance.

According to Kabbalah, we are called to heal the world and save the Divine. The world is always in peril. When we keep listening in our dreams and our lives, we may be able to discern how we are each pointed to ever greater wholeness, thus having a hand in healing the world. We are daily being asked to clean our own little corner of our lives, of the world. This ordinary work, from taking ownership of our messes, to being a volunteer on a palliative care team, is holy work.

Loving Anybody Is Loving God

One of Jung's fine teachings was that long-term relationships are excellent—and often challenging—containers for transformation. Psychological and spiritual change may occur when anyone in a partnership—or in any family or other social system—begins to awaken in some way. When just one person begins to change, it is almost inevitable that the whole social system will be stretched, and more consciousness for all may be the outcome.

I ask my six whether they have intentional *shmutz*-cleaning practices. Although they all use different words and have different perspectives, the answer is a resounding yes. Squeaky clean is not possible or even the goal, but if we're awake, it's a bit easier to become aware of how we mess up, to be more conscious and thoughtful. In the Jewish tradition, the month of *Elul* is seen as a time to search one's heart and soul in preparation for the High Holy Days of Rosh Hashanah, the New Year, and Yom Kippur, the Day of Atonement. The ten days between Rosh Hashanah and Yom Kippur are called the Days of Awe, when we're supposed to pull out all the stops in looking at our sins. This is in prepa-

Chapter 3: Doing the Work

ration for Yom Kippur, the day we're ostensibly either written in the Book of Life, or not. I like the Hebrew word *chata*, which means "sin" or "missing the mark." When we sin, we miss the mark and we can try again. And again. I see *shmutz*-cleaning as a daily imperative, not just during the Days of Awe. That said, I seldom get bull's-eyes. "We all have *mishegas* [craziness]," a friend once told me cheerfully when I was feeling a bit holy about all my hard work of waking up. "And sometimes," he continued, "it is the most interesting aspect of us."

    Alan is my helpmeet as I awaken to existence. In the continuing spirit of disclosure, a few bread-and-butter examples: Too frequently I'm already talking enthusiastically as I walk through the door of Alan's office, without paying attention to whether he is engaged in his own work. I am bossy and controlling. I go on for too long when he has clearly had enough of my ruminating. I offer too many suggestions and opinions. (As my friend Susie taught me, advice and opinions are usually for the speaker, not the listener.) I almost always take the biggest piece of pie or cake—even on Shabbat—unless I am feeling a bit holy. I am heir to my familial proclivity of self-righteousness and finger-wagging. I have a know-it-all judgmental shadow, and sometimes forget to keep my mouth shut. Lovely. And while I hardly need to be shot at dawn for these acts, they are ways I am not attuned to Alan, my beloved. If conscious or mindful, I will notice his small sigh or change in breathing. Alan generally has a tolerant temperament and seldom tells me to take a hike, which makes the work of waking up and being responsible that much harder. If I look in the mirror in these microcosmic moments, as well as in those bigger times when we get into trouble or conflict, I can listen with an open heart. Then I may be able to drop my defenses and explanations, get into Alan's boat, and be his friend. I can also continue my lifelong work of waking up to how the wounds and inheritances of my childhood may show up in unkind or selfish ways. The ways I can become a better mother are infinite, and I receive lessons on how to do so, by our children, somewhat regularly. I know, too, that loving sometimes means saying no, being tough and challenging. Loving anybody is loving God. That's really what it's all about.

Chapter 3: Doing the Work

Close to the Ground

A return to the reverence for air, water, and soil, would be a good place to start.
—Arthur Green, Ehyeh: A Kabbalah for Tomorrow

All of it.

Dried garlic stalks, brittle
from summer drought.
Farmer in his khakis—torn
pants, cracked boots.
Dusty beard.

Fat crickets scurry, disturbed
as we unearth Israeli garlic bulbs,
arrogant with life, despite
the long, hot summer.

Mandy, James, Ethan.
Maybe mainly
Mandy. Her eyes shine,
voice firm and clear.
A teaching

moment for
her five-year old—

*Close to the ground,
James. Pull the stalks
close to the ground.*

Sweeping the Room

It may help to wake up if the room is not a huge mess, cluttered with piles of books, pens, unread papers, crotchety files, old journals in spiral-bound notebooks, countless photos. I speak metaphorically, of course. Some people are naturally spiritually tidier than others. I think "forest people" may be more organized than "tree people." I'm a tree person, and usually get lost in the moment, absorbed by the thought, book, or person with whom I'm engaged. There are times when seeing only the tree is precisely what the sacredness of the moment desires, such as in deep personal work, being a spiritual companion, or when pausing on a walk to pay respects to a newly blossomed rose. But it helps to see the forest, to have an overall plan and be organized, especially with regard to time. I have been arguing with time as long as I can remember.

As a spiritual director, I sweep my room by preparing for the work. I try to take care of my mind, body, heart, and soul. I pray, read, write, sit in silence for my mind and soul. I do daily Pilates for my body and walk daily for about an hour unless the weather makes it completely impossible. For my heart, I listen to my emotions and allow them full expression where appropriate. Emotions are generally asking for attention and need discerning respect. One of my directees tells me she wants to learn to listen to the sacred more deeply. I tell her that being still and very quiet for a long while can help. I also say that, for some people, the opposite is true; they can connect deeply with themselves and the Holy One while engaged in some intense activity. The goal is to encounter the memories, conflicts, and emotions that have been waiting for us in our psyche. It may be difficult at times. But if we don't defend ourselves in countless possible ways, and listen deeply to our hearts, it becomes more likely that we will be able to hear from the Divine. My directee says, looking a bit fearful, "But what if there is nothing inside?" "There is Nothing inside," I say and give her a mini-tour of Jewish mysticism and the grand No-thing, the Holy One, who is, after all, directing the traffic.

In Jewish mysticism we learn about the different attributes of the Holy One and how sometimes we need compassion and sometimes firmness in our lives—often both. We work on becoming conscious, on befriending the less-than-perfectly-neat aspects of ourselves as well as the more adorable parts. Sweeping the room is another form of discernment. The further down I can go into my body, the more I am able to feel sadness or fear. I'm not so great at allowing my angry feelings, so anger may get stopped up in my mind and my body. Work in progress. Talking to someone when I am in distress is a way to sweep my room. Big thoughts and feelings—maybe even medium-sized thoughts and feelings—welcome witness, safe space held by another. Sweeping the room is a way of being present, of moving from just our minds into our hearts, our bodies, so we may become more openhearted in listening to life, to the sacred. I sometimes write letters to God when I'm confused, and the simple pouring out of all that is within leaves me clearer and usually more at peace. God listens.

Nothing Is Only Itself

We turn to the only reality that seems to make sense: the sphere of ourselves. But that too is a sinkhole.
—Michael Fishbane, Fragile Finitude

It's not your poetry
or whether your granola
is good this time,
pecans and all.

Not the thank-you note,
the song sprung free.
Even your love.

Nothing is only itself.
Everything is everything.

You will remember
and forget this
as many times
as you smile
or frown.

You will think
this is the answer to my pain
and forget
it is only one bread crumb
out of the forest.

You will read a book

on mysticism,
do fifty push-ups,
think you're hot.

And if you were inclined
to tattoos,
I might suggest
Nothing
is only itself
on the underbelly
of your left forearm,

and

Everything
is Everything,
on your right.

Rituals

In 1992 and 1993, the Toronto Blue Jays won the World Series. Toronto is a city that loves sports, and almost everyone was completely obsessed with the playoffs. At the time, Glen, our second son, was twenty-two, and Daniel, our youngest, seventeen. Eli, the oldest, had left home already. The guys are wild about sports, and the championship season was nail-biting heaven for the whole family. In those days we had a small vegetable patch in the back of our home, which produced very little other than a few seriously disturbed-looking cucumbers and one outrageously large zucchini that was chosen to become the mascot and good-luck charm for the Jays. There were strict rules to be followed. Indeed, winning the World Series was entirely dependent on the Hoffmann family of Balmoral Avenue. The zucchini was placed on a table facing the television at an angle, slightly to the left. It had to be in exactly the same position for every single game. The zuke wore a red-and-white hat knitted by Dan when he was in his knitting phase. (He only knew purl stitch, and the hat, like the cukes, was somewhat deformed.) One of the boys had to have his hand on the zuke at crucial moments in the game or the Blue Jays were in danger of not scoring or not striking out the Atlanta Braves hotshot at the home plate. We won the World Series two years in a row.

People engage in rituals with the intention of achieving a wide array of desired outcomes, from reducing anxiety to boosting confidence, alleviating grief, or performing well in competition. Rituals help people contain emotions that sometimes feel too large to manage. They create boundaries and can foster a sense of safety. Rituals can deepen and enrich an experience profoundly. Many of us may have family rituals that warm and amuse us when we remember them: Our family played Trivial Pursuits for years in the waning hours of Yom Kippur, the Day of Atonement, when we were all fasting and serious grumpiness was lurking.

When I went daily for five weeks to the hospital for radiation for my colon cancer treatment, I always used the blue cotton bag I had received at a Spiritual Directors International conference. In the bag were a bottle with exactly the two glasses of water I was required to drink before each treatment, my health and hospital cards, a crossword puzzle, a novel, a pen and pencil, a notebook, some gloves and a hat, and a dark chocolate caramel for after the treatment. By using the blue bag as a sacred object, I felt accompanied by my clan, those who have a home in the world of spiritual companionship. Each night before the next treatment, I prepared my bag. I am not usually so well organized, but this ritual felt comforting and even a bit holy to me.

We Are Consciousness Trying to Become Aware of Itself

My friend Beth works as a psychotherapist in a large community practice. She is considering quitting to go into private practice. She does not have a great deal of money saved but feels an intense call to leave public practice. She's in discernment, she tells me. Since she is not a "spiritual type," I ask her what this means. "Sitting with my uncertainty," she says. "Asking the question many times in my mind—stay or leave? Noticing which answer comes more often. Thinking about money. Independence." I tell Beth that she reminds me of a dream I once had: *It is time to remain empty and wait for the new to emerge.*

In a life of discernment, we may ask, "What do you want

of me, Holy One? What now, my Love? Should I watch that YouTube video? Respond to that group email? Quit my job in the community practice? Go for a walk before writing?" We may ask, "How do You want me to love You? Is baking homemade granola more important than meditating or writing? Do I go to the soup kitchen, volunteer for Meals on Wheels, or spend more time with my kids?" *God guides from within*, a dream told me. And when we believe we receive an answer from the Beloved, are we hallucinating? Maybe. When I was in training to become a spiritual director, one of my fellow trainees asked the teachers how we were to *know* if we were indeed hearing God. We don't, they told us. We follow the guidance that seems to be rising to the top of the heap and then pay attention to the fruits of our choice. Or as one of my dreams asked and then answered, *Is the guidance from God or from me? It doesn't matter if there are good results.* (I opted for the granola. Pecans, pistachios, and maple syrup; lime zest and a good shake of salt are my secret ingredients.)

In Kabbalah we learn that the Divine is always evolving. In our yearning to become more whole, we are consciousness trying to become aware of itself. In this way we assist the Holy One. Or, said more simply, God needs us to help God wake up.

I Don't Know

I have a sudden inspiration: Reach out to Adam. We come from the same country and although I don't know him well, I hear he's generous and kind. I want to talk with him about my "walk into a room" dream and my time of dread. I'm told he's wise and super deep, and I know he has written oceans about Jewish mysticism. Plus, he's a big-shot rabbi and may have a

Chapter 3: Doing the Work

secret or two to share. I wonder if the idea is God-inspired, then tell myself to knock it off. Just write. Adam responds promptly and offers to have a Zoom meeting. I am thrilled.

I am so happy to see Adam, I tell him when we meet the next day on Zoom. He is kind. I feel it immediately. After a little catch-up, I tell Adam my dream. He listens carefully and asks, "Did the dream say, 'unity'?" Yes.

"The dream is interesting," he says after a while, "but I don't really know what to make of it. I am not a dream person, as you seem to be." There is a moment or two of silence, then Adam smiles, "I *can* say I see God as Y-H-W-H, as the One who is, was, and will be."

We agree on this. The Holy One is always in process.

"Let me tell you of my time of dread then, Adam," I say, not one to give up. I offer a detailed description of the strange four-month period where I felt deep dread that seemed quite alien, quite "other." I tell Adam how I worked like the devil to "fix myself," seeking all sorts of help, to no avail. The time of dread had arrived suddenly and left just as suddenly. I share how I became even more familiar with my own dark shadow, how I worked with the fear of dying. I say that my sense of the Divine, always in flight, was upended even more. I pause, then add with a little flourish, "And two weeks after the dread left, my colon cancer was diagnosed. Some say God was warning me about what was coming up. Some even say I was meeting the dark side of God. What do you think, Adam?"

"Honestly, Jinks," Adam says kindly, "I don't know. There are just some things I don't think we can know. Maybe that is beautiful, too. But I am sorry to disappoint you."

My eyes fill with tears, not of disappointment but "being touched" tears, God-tears, I tell Adam. I am so moved by his humility, his integrity. He's a big shot and he simply says he doesn't know.

"Ah," I say, "*now I have something to tell.*" I tell Adam about my other huge dream: *I am to row alone to an island on God's holy day, the thirteenth, to plant seeds of uncertainty and unknowing.*

"This I can get my teeth into," Adam smiles. "Uncertainty and unknowing. That feels about the right way to talk about Y-H-W-H, the One."

CHAPTER 4: WAKING UP

Riding Shotgun

The only place you have to travel to find God's word is to your own heart. The journey to the heart is the mystical quest.
—Arthur Green, *Ehyeh: A Kabbalah for Tomorrow*

To call it a journey
suggests
a "there."
There is no "there."
Only here, now,
in and down,
toward the center
of your heart.

Buckle up.

The good news—
you
are in the passenger seat
of the grand automobile,
and your attention
can wander.

The bad news?
You are in the *passenger* seat.

To get closer to the ever-

moving One,
prepare to meet
yourself—
in the many ways
your childhood woes,
the nasties
of life,
and mystery
show up.

The ride is exhilarating.

Sometimes.

    At other times,

like riding
a Mustang bareback
in the wilds,
howling
wolves close by.

You may learn
a few things.

Or not.
So,

have salve handy,
wear good shoes,
and pack

a good helping
of salted nuts,
a crisp apple
and a granola
bar.

Stop the Rocking

The spiritual director moves his chair from across the room and sits next to Betsy. Mature and sensible, Betsy has been meeting with Harry for several years. She rocks her chair back and forth rhythmically. Complete silence. Harry, too, says nothing. After several moments of quiet except for Betsy's rocking, Harry puts his foot on the base of the chair. The chair is stopped. More silence. After a few moments Betsy covers her face and begins to weep quietly. Harry's quiet empathic presence says volumes. After a long while Betsy turns to look at Harry. "I don't understand. We will soon be moving to our new home. It is a beautiful house. I want to move. But I feel sad. How can I feel sad about a choice we made with consciousness and joy?"

"Tell me about the home you'll be leaving," Harry says kindly, "the neighborhood, the friends you've made over the years." Betsy begins weeping again. "How can I feel two things at once?" Betsy asked. "Because you're human," Harry replies.

Now Is the Time...

In 1979 I had another of my very bossy, directive dreams, which told me, *Now is the time for your Jungian analysis.* I knew nothing about Carl Jung or that many Jungian analysts use dreams as their primary modus operandi. What a miracle that the Dream Maker spoke so clearly—a direct wake-up call.

A young psychotherapist at the time, I had been invited to present a workshop on Gestalt therapy at a large psychotherapy conference. After my presentation, I attended a small seminar on Jungian analysis. At lunch that day, I joked to my friends about going into Jungian analysis because the presenter,

Chapter 4: Waking Up

Fraser Boa, a former movie star and director, was absurdly handsome. Soon after the conference, I remembered the dream and contacted Fraser. Within minutes of meeting him, I *knew*. I did not know what he had, but I wanted it, too. Fraser was utterly present, focused, authentic. He had gravitas and a clear, still manner, unlike anything I had ever experienced. He was guided by and connected to his unconscious, to what Jungians call the Godhead, although I did not know that then. Carl Jung wrote that an encounter with the numinous is the essence of the healing experience. Working with dreams is working with the Holy of Holies. I began analysis with Fraser soon after, and I have been connected to the world of dreams and Jungian depth psychology ever since.

Silenced by the Eternal

We meet the God-bestowed world with mind and body.
   —Michael Fishbane, Fragile Finitude

This morning a walk on the beach—
a little boy with no bathing suit
is having an intense conversation with shells and sand
fleas. His mom, belly over red bikini,
calls to his dad, "Come and see what
he's doing. Come and see."

Tonight, a Halloween party—"Sue
has Alzheimer's," John says sweetly.
"Loves
to dance, though. We've still got
the moves." Indeed, they have.
Her salsa swing has sureness
and sweet rhythm, so different
from her awkward walk
back to the table.

The bartender pours
with two hands, slinging limes
and wisecracks. Jokes
older than the hills.

Now, an old man, gold
chain around neck,
gray hairs
on well-worn chest, pulls

his wife
closer, croons
Dance me to the End of Love.

I study God as I walk
through the portals
of my life—my heart
blown
to smithereens
by fleeting glimpses
of the Eternal. For some, it is sunsets
or Schubert. For me, humans.

Sometimes even "thank You" won't
cut it. For there are no
words. Only silence.
Or, perhaps
those of a mother,
calling, "Come, come and see."

It's Happening Again

In my early teens, I read a book by the prolific British writer Colin Wilson in which he wrote of hitchhiking through the town of St. Neot in Britain and having a sudden and startling epiphany. Becoming acutely present and "wildly enthusiastic" about everything he was seeing and hearing, Wilson realized that most of his life was spent in "debilitating indifference." As he scribbled the phrase "St. Neot margin" in the novel he was reading, he vowed to devote his life to living in an awakened state.

I had no way, then, to discern why "St. Neot margin" brought tears to my eyes. I did not understand that I had been spun momentarily awake. It took many years to recognize what had been so startling. I have spent my life learning about and putting into practice—at least a little—what Colin Wilson described. He was the first person who helped me know that the Divine could be experienced in the ordinary ways of life. I do not remember if he even spoke of God.

Many of us sleepwalk through our days. The spiritual practice of waking up "on the way" is the intention to study God as we move through our days. Every moment is a mother lode of instruction if we pay attention. If we know this, we will sometimes experience great wonder, great awe, great joy. Also, great sorrow, great terror, great dread.

Alan and I are on vacation in Hilton Head Island in South Carolina. One of the ways I experience the sacred in life is through food and wine. We are dining at the Santa Fe Café. The food is perfect—blackened redfish with rice and black beans, garlic, and coriander. A perfectly rare, juicy T-bone steak with chili-infused onion rings. Bread pudding for dessert, covered in a white chocolate sauce with more than a splash of bourbon.

My favorite white wine, a New Zealand Sauvignon Blanc. We always share everything—get to taste more this way. Not much conversation, a few ecstatic groans. Sated, I look to my left. There are eight people at the table, an older man at the head. There is obvious warmth and familiarity in the group—likely a family celebration. And suddenly, one of my St. Neot moments. It is as if the sun has just blazed into the fashionably darkened restaurant. I become intensely aware of the padded leather of my chair, the way the air blesses my cheeks, how my breathing slows. Noise abates. Everything is larger than life and at the same time pinpointed, shot through with light. Each person is bold, clear, and separate and yet there is an unmistakable oneness. The moment feels oddly eternal, despite its inherent transience. I have entered that place of time out of time, or perhaps I have entered the eternal now. I am stilled by gratitude, flooded with tenderness for the complete strangers I behold.

"It's happening again," I whisper to Alan, "I am recognizing the ongoing blessed mystery of creation."

In moments like this, I know—as much as one can know the Divine—that all people are of the oneness that is God. Everyone has a story, a life of successes and failures, longings, joys, challenges, troubles, and triumphs. Everyone has a body and soul; dreams they remember or do not. Toenails and nostril hairs. And when "it happens," I am present to the moment, continuous with life. My interiority is outside and the Beloved is as if transparent. The wonder I feel is almost overwhelming. I am in a field of love, so much bigger than I. In Hebrew you might call this *ahava raba*— "great love."

Abraham Joshua Heschel said, "Indifference to wonder is the source of all sin." Walking my days with the intention of being awake, as well as committing to my daily spiritual practices, makes it more likely that I will have such moments. But the intense *presence* I experience in the restaurant happens to me. I cannot make these blessed moments occur. While all life is sacred, my experience is often grace.

In the Santa Fe Café, Alan smiles. He is familiar with my ecstasy in such blessed moments. And since he and I are committed to a life of both/and, after a decent while he chuckles and reminds me of our lunch at a Cracker Barrel restaurant while traveling to beautiful Hilton Head. I had said of a family of four where the parents were fighting, the children grumbling, the father yelling at the little boy with the dirty face, and the mother not looking up from her iPhone, "Sometimes it's hard to believe that everything is God."

Horizon

Liberation is where light breaks through, and the horizon changes.
—Michael Fishbane, Fragile Finitude

Keep my eye
on the goal—
those gray trees,
elephant shapes
at the horizon.
        Distant
hills of purple plums.
Something akin
to a dwarf smokestack.

But it is hopeless.

Right here,
    in this place,
my feet insist
on a Jewish jig—
      quickstep right
          left   tumble
     back
          and   forth
       arms   flung   wide
    mouth a perfect O—
serenade to this
bare brown
patch of ground.

        And to my right,
a green, thorny bush
on fire without
being consumed.

Not Yet Speech Ripe*

To pray is to choose...to notice that presence.
　—Arthur Green, An Addendum on Prayer

All you can do is tilt
your axis
　　slightly to the left,
listen,
look
for the murmuring

lift
your eyes
to where flocks
of gulls
ply the skies, fly

this way,
then that—flow
from
black
to white and back
again.

You almost hear
the sound
of wings that brush
the sky, so soft, a sigh.
No words yet

for the catch
in your throat, the tears
that pierce
your eyes, your heart
which tumbles yes.

On the waterfront
a little girl holds a tiny shell
and says "Daddy,
look."
And all Daddy can do
is lift high the girl
    the shell and
        murmur
            "my..."

*Not yet speech ripe: A phrase used by Jeremy Taylor, an expert on dreams.

Pause

At a Spiritual Directors International conference in Boston many years ago, I heard a story by the Reverend Kirk Jones that I'll never forget. One evening, Wynton Marsalis was playing a trumpet blues melody in a nightclub, "You're Gonna Miss Me When I'm Gone." The solo was more and more haunting, the weeping notes calling the audience closer and closer. Marsalis was a breath from the last bar when someone's cell phone rang. An absurd musical jingle of "Smile and the Whole World Smiles with You" shattered the mood. The audience snickered, then laughed, then roared, then began chattering. Marsalis had lost them just before he had brought his evocative creation home.

What did Marsalis do? He paused for several moments, breathed, and then, listening to the deepest wisdom in himself, turned to his audience and began playing "Smile and the Whole World Smiles with You." He played several different versions, riffing on the old chestnut. The audience grew quieter and quieter. After a while, Marsalis returned to "You're Gonna Miss Me When I'm Gone." The melody lifted into the nightclub, haunting once more, but different from his first version. The audience was rapt. When he came to the last lingering note, people leapt to their feet.

Pausing is not necessarily silence. Pausing is being present in the moment and listening for the Voice of all that is. Pausing can help us wake up and relate to what is deeply alive, what is called for in the moment.

The Spinning You Feel

Time as it is ordinarily experienced it is an illusion.
—Sanford Drob, Kabbalistic Visions

Dawn. Faint hues of pink,
mirrored
silver and navy.
The ocean seems hardly
to breathe.
Sea-wash caresses the shore
with a humble hum. Then

your neighbor intrudes
on your reverie—
loud curse and slam
of the door. Smell
of bitter coffee, burnt
toast.

The gardener, six floors below, roars
into cheerful action; his machine
whacking weeds and silence
into stubble.

All that exists
comes into being
and dissolves

on this morning, now fully aroused.

This may well be the cause
of the spinning
you feel as your pen's ink dashes
across the page
scribbling
its love letter to the Holy.

Ocean, neighbor, coffee, burnt toast, gardener—
all simply part
of the story
that began before
the Spirit of God
moved upon the face
of the ocean's
breath-held stillness at dawn.

Jinks Will Be Dead at Seventy-Four

At seventy-three I had a dream telling me I would be dead at seventy-four. As a recovering hypochondriac, my sensitivity to real or imagined physical symptoms continues to be one of my beloved and cursed calls to wake up. Feeling very clever, I chose to work with the dream as another invitation to surrender. I wondered if it was inviting more death of my ego, my self-image, more relinquishing of the notion that I was driving the bus. A lifetime's work. The dream came when we were in our winter home of Marco Island, Florida. A couple of days later, I was walking on the beach when I saw a little girl running to her dad. "Daddy, Daddy!" she said, holding a shell in her sweet, plump, opened hand, "Look at this!" Daddy, who had been paying keen attention to her all this time, responded in a voice ringing with liveliness and enthusiasm, "Whatcha got? Whatcha got?" I was stopped dead in my tracks by the Spirit so radiant in the little girl, her dad, even the shell.

In a spiritual friendship conversation later that week, I related the story. "It was so beautiful, dear Pam, I *just died*," I said. I heard my words. So did Pam. I shed a few tears of wonder. "Maybe if Jinks is at least a little dead," I said, "there is more room for God." I told Pam of my *dead at seventy-four* dream.

I am sorry to tell that after the *Whatcha got* experience, I was more than a little full of myself. "This is it," I decided. "I must be pretty enlightened." But the Trickster is clever, and later that night he rubbed my nose in my so-not-dead ego. I had a stupid fight with Alan after I became authoritative and know-it-all about a friend. I was full of prescriptions on how she should deal with a tough situation. Alan told me to knock it off—three times. The same night I dreamed I was wearing a long, heavy topcoat, the kind that generals wear in the army—at least in movies. The coat was covered in medals and was so heavy I tipped face forward onto the floor. If we allow ourselves to surrender to life, our egos will die, just a little. This is an ongoing challenge. And while our egos need to die, they also do not. This is mysticism for you. The ego is how we engage with the Self, with the Holy One of All Being. And God, as we keep saying, demands feisty engagement. The blessed both/and. This ego/Self thing is a pretty big deal in psychospiritual work—sometimes we win the toss of the coin, sometimes we lose. But the truth is that if we cooperate with the desire life has for us, we win.

The capacity to hold and own the opposites and contradictions in life and in our psyches is fundamental to spiritual maturity and helps carve out more of our wholeness. In the course of a lifetime, an individual will encounter sparks within his or her own soul and in the world that only he or she can redeem. When we are in connection with the flow of divinity, we are more likely to have an ethical, moral orientation to life. We seem to notice beauty more frequently, and we are kinder in our relationships and even with ourselves. Yet there is always the war between good and evil in the psyche of humankind, and some say in the Divine. I "died" twice at the *Whatcha got* time: once from ecstasy, once from foolishness.

Alan told me recently, "I'm eighty, and I will never get it right." God bless the man.

Alex, and How Our Stories Can Run Us

I have known Alex since we were kids in South Africa. We don't meet often, but when we do, we get down to it. Clearly strong in character, he is quiet and reserved, disinclined to assert himself or ask for assistance or attention. I have long intuited that there is more warmth and expansiveness in his large, bony body than is evident. One night we go for dinner to a new Italian restaurant in the neighborhood and linger for over two hours on the restaurant's new outdoor patio. (I might add that we polish off a bottle of luscious red wine.) Alex is unusually open this night, and I comment that there is more tiger under his skin than people might think. He becomes quiet, and after a while, somewhat uncharacteristically, begins musing about his childhood. He had been a very curious, openhearted child, he says, but his mother, insecure and chronically depressed, often pushed away his affectionate hugs. Alex looks away. "And then there was my teacher in grade school," he continues. "I was enthusiastic and confident as a child. Always waving my arm in the air because I knew the answers to questions. I loved school and learning." The teacher reprimanded Alex one day, told him to leave space for the other children to respond. "I never raised my hand again," he says quietly.

My heart is sore. As a child, Alex had a lively, loving spirit that had not been cherished or witnessed with joy. Indeed, he had been rebuffed and shamed. He did what perhaps most of us would—went underground to avoid being hurt. Knowing Alex, I don't expect that he will change dramatically after our dinner, for it is unusual for people to have personality transplants. I hope I am wrong. But Alex has allowed me in, and I think it is possible that, in the future, the connection between us may become more righteous in a certain sense. Not righteous in the holy-holy way but in right relationship with ourselves and each other—more open, intimate, immediate.

The Throbbing of Divine Everlastingness*

Every moment pours forth a distinct flood of phenomena and possibilities—and everything depends on how we respond.
—Michael Fishbane, Jewish Hermeneutical Theology

Perhaps this is the miracle—

that we can awaken
yawn
stretch
rise from our beds
wash our faces
brush our teeth

can open windows
unlock doors
toast the six-grain
bread
cut tomatoes
in thick
juicy
slices

and
every moment
of our blessed lives—

do not fall down
in mute wonder.

*Phrase used by Michael Fishbane.

Whatever Is True in Our Psyche, So Is the Opposite—in the Divine, Too

It says in the Torah that we are made b'tzelem Elohim, in the image of God. I suspect that in rare moments of wholeness, we stand balanced on the boundary of light and dark, of unity. In this place, we know in the same moment terror and wonder, dread and awe. In these moments, we are awake.

I have never met anybody who is not a mix of bright and dark shadow, good and bad, love and hate, blessed wounds and radiant health. One of the people I work with in spiritual direction is extremely polite, almost timid. Mabel is reluctant to assert her needs in sessions and tells me that she is often fearful. Surprisingly, she reports frequent altercations with strangers, store clerks, people in the service industry, other car drivers. Mabel is learning to have compassion for herself as she becomes more familiar with her imperious, demanding shadow. As she gets to know herself more, she becomes more respectfully assertive. She becomes aware of her lack of consideration. As we plumb her depths, Mabel understands more all the time why she is fearful and timid. She grieves for the girl who received so little attention from her imperious, demanding, impatient parents. In our work, she finds, too, a healthy voice that is angry.

Whatever is true about us in our psyche, so is the opposite. When we know and incorporate this truth, it gradually becomes possible to accept, contain, and not act out our dark shadow. We may learn also to embrace our light shadow—those shining unrealized parts of ourselves, such as absurd humor or huge, generous love. When we take a long, loving look at the real, as the Jesuit theologian Walter Burghardt famously described the act of contemplation, we enter into holy relationship with the Beloved and become more authentic, more fully ourselves.

God Rescues Us and Vice Versa

We're having family Shabbat dinner—crispy, spicy roast chicken with spring asparagus, rosemary potatoes, salad. Alan and our guys are talking sports. They always do. The subject tonight is people who have made comebacks. "What about Serena?" I throw in, eager to be part of the conversation. "She won the French Open ten months after having her baby." I've hooked them. Any offering about sports does. Not so much if I talk about spiritual matters. We talk about how exultant Serena must have been. "Victories are temporary," I point out. "But I am fortunate because I am on the biggest adventure every day, in my daily game of tennis with the Source of Wisdom. Win or lose, I always learn something." I go on to explain how a dream about tennis could be a metaphor for relationship, for the ball is hit back and forth between two or more players. "In my case, God and me," I say, and wax on, now exultant about dreams as a wake-up call. I throw into the conversation one of my very favorite tiny, big dreams: *Search for the Living Spirit*. All my guys nod, a bit distractedly. They've heard my sermon before. Glen stifles a yawn.

At the end of the 1990s romantic-comedy *Pretty Woman*, we get a fresh spin on *tikkun ha-olam*, the healing of the world. The story centers on a down-on-her-luck Hollywood prostitute, Vivian (Julia Roberts), who is hired by the wealthy Edward Lewis (Richard Gere) to be his escort for several business and social functions. As the movie progresses, we realize that over the course of her weeklong stay with him—oldest and sweetest story in the world—Vivian and Edward have become smitten.

The rather corny but charming story is drawing to an end. On the way to the airport, Edward rethinks his life and has the hotel chauffeur detour to Vivian's apartment building. "Vivian!" he yells. "Vivian!" She comes to the window of her tenth-floor apartment and looks out. With a newly purchased bunch of red roses between his teeth, and an obvious fear of heights, Edward begins the climb on the fire escape.

Vivian descends. They meet midway.

"What happens," Edward asks, "after the man climbs up the tower to rescue the woman?"

Flashing her trademark grin, Julia Roberts as Vivian replies, "She rescues him right back."

If God is everything and the source of everything, when we are rescued by the Divine, we need to turn right around and rescue God back. How does God rescue us? The Divine breathes life into us and offers us countless opportunities to become more conscious, more responsible, kinder every blessed moment of our lives. God rescues us by making creation so impossibly beautiful we should walk around in a state of constant prayer for the miracle of existence. God reminds us—in a thought that arrives suddenly—to pause, to listen to the thrum of life, inside and out. God rescues us by offering opportunities for healing when life goes swimmingly and when it doesn't.

How do we rescue the Holy One right back? Creation, like us, is a work in progress. The work of *tikkun ha-nefesh* in the service of *tikkun ha-olam*, the healing of our souls in the service of the healing of the world, serves the Holy One as we do our holy waking-up practice, in whatever form it takes. Anytime we serve the world by kindness or activism—by picking up trash from city streets, for example—we rescue God. Although we are less than one-eighty-millionth of one crumb in creation, we are nonetheless responsible for other crumbs, and our love needs to be expressed in action. When we take homemade soup to a shut-in neighbor, when we think twice and three times before we speak when steam is coming from our ears, we rescue the Beloved. Our help is always needed, for as it says in Psalm 90, the Divine does not have hands, but we do.

CHAPTER 5: ENCOUNTERING THE LIGHT

What We Once Knew

All we seek to learn is what we as children once knew in the Garden.
—Lawrence Kushner, River of Light

No way to tell the tale of that moment—
the miracle, all fingers and toes, a shock
of black hair, and you two, so blonde.
Your husband mute in wonder.

He's the first baby boy in a flock of girls.
The angels surely touched him
above his lip right before birth,
the time when the boundary
between worlds is not yet sealed,
and final secrets are told.

You whisper in his ear, tiny whorl
of perfect seashell because you want
him to remember what he learned,
so he can tell you,
                when he can speak.

You cry with your husband
later that first day. You cannot
believe you asked him, you say,
but that baby, you say,
                he smiled.

Sometimes Shadow Is the Way In

Alan and I met in South Africa when he was nineteen, and I, sixteen. He was my best friend's boyfriend. One December, when my best friend was away on vacation with her family, Alan invited me to a film. This was not an invitation from a place of purity or holiness. I accepted enthusiastically. This, too, a response from the less-than-pure side of soul. I took the train into Johannesburg, the big city, where Alan met me at the station. We went to His Majesty's Theatre to see the film *Around the World in Eighty Days*. About halfway through, Alan took my hand. Lord! I held onto his hand with all my life, for something remarkable was happening, and we both felt it. It was not just the simmering eroticism of two young people. We had both betrayed the same person and remarkably the Great Mystery pierced our souls in that very moment—with both light and dark shadow. Although we did not know it then, our love, the future of our shared lives, and our paths to individuation were born at the boundary of light and dark.

We married a few years later. My ex-best friend was not at the wedding.

Most humans enter a romantic relationship unconsciously looking to the other to heal their brokenness. To be born means we will be broken. A small or large rent. Life will tear us. A long-term relationship offers the opportunity to love your partner as they are, to put aside your own needs and be openhearted and empty of your own agenda—at least some of the time. In the early days, your partner may seem close to perfection. This state of projection, of rose-colored glasses, generally lasts at least a couple of years. But as time goes on, you will notice that she is way too fussy about tidiness. He procrastinates, so you often must wait for him. He has multiple excuses for any annoying behavior, and she snorts when she laughs, just like her mother. The rose-colored glasses are off, and these are just the small "things" in a relationship. Now you have the opportunity to really love. It's part of the job description of a long-term relationship, and good loving takes forever. But in those precious moments when you are able to see the unique story in the other's soul, the love you feel may be transformative, almost too much to bear. This is love as spiritual practice.

Neither Alan nor I are perfect. Far from it. He is superbly "good enough" in the parlance of the British psychoanalyst Donald Winnicott. I am a bundle of trouble too many times. But we were given a lifelong task. As I see it, God shot an arrow through our hearts in His Majesty's Theatre and said, "Go to it, you two. Get to know each other, yourselves, life, and do your best to be kind." Ours is an ordinary story. A love story. An opportunity to keep awakening to the imperfection and the holiness of life and love.

In an intimate, authentic relationship, where we are present—without defenses, in vulnerability—we enter an alchemical vessel where both may be transformed. And God might have continued, "Learn about love through each other, and then go out and be *menschen* [decent people] in the world."

Relationship also offers the opportunity to love an imperfect Divine, who, like us, is still in the process of becoming. Jewish mysticism posits that God's love for us and ours for God are one and the same thing. In learning to love another, we are learning to love the Source of Life.

Alan, as mirror to the many ways I need to become more conscious and kinder, has been, and continues to be, the instrument to awaken me to love. His very difference from me is the

whetstone against which I am sharpened into presence. I am always learning more about blessing, then dissolving my expectations, for they surely are premeditated resentments, as it is taught in the Twelve Step Program.
And then I get to love him, others, and life more.

Beginnings, Middles, and Moving toward the Finish Line

It was our fifty-fifth wedding anniversary in December 2019. Each year Alan writes a poem to mark the day. The poem has evolved into a chronicle of the family history, a nod to the significant events of the year, or, to put it another way, a love poem to the immediate, rather large family. This is not any love poem: It is tender, irreverent, poignant, and sprinkled liberally with humorous Yiddish, all done in more or less perfect rhyme. Several stanzas. As the family has grown, so have the poems. Alan works on his creation for a couple of days. It may be the best gift I receive each year. When I read it—first silently, then aloud—I always laugh and cry. Laughter and tears, a good summary of our marriage and our love for over sixty years. Tears of worry, grief, remorse, gratitude. Tears of overwhelming tenderness and love. This year the poem was a whammy, for I had been diagnosed with my second cancer, and since surgery was slated for 2020, my future was a bit iffy.

When Eli, the oldest, was forty-eight, he called from Israel. Alan and I were in Florida, our winter home. Eli told us that he planned to make a detour to Marco Island after one of his business trips to New York. A rare treat, given his busyness and fifteen children. Eli was a *ba-al t'shuvah*, which means literally "someone who has returned to God." He was drawn, at sixteen, to becoming a Chasid, a member of a sect of Orthodox Judaism characterized by religious zeal and a spirit of joy, prayer, and charity. We immediately invited his brothers to join in the adventure—sans wives. No children, either. A reunion. The five of us would be alone for the first time in twenty-six years. Glen and Daniel sprang themselves free, and the five of us had a profound and unforgettable four days. Walks on the beach. Conversations in twos, threes, and fives. Long meals. Boggle. (I never won, even though Dan gave me extra lessons.) Shabbat. Eli and Dan played golf with Alan. Glen and I talked for two and a half hours. Without interruption. Some excellent crying, too.

Eli, Glen, and Dan all caused the requisite amount of trouble when they were growing up. As with all experiences of waking up, the tuition for Alan and me was not always pleasant. But, fortunately for us, the good news significantly outweighed the bad. We certainly had times of worry, but, prior to Eli's death, there was never anything completely impossible to deal with. I loved them passionately as babies and little ones, and despite knowing that unconditional love is the ideal, I failed at that, and especially when aliens inhabited their bodies as adolescents. In Florida, once again I was wildly in love with them. Watching them as we ate dinner, there were moments when I had an almost physical ache for them to be little boys again so I might hold them in my arms, smooth their blond hair as they slept, chase them around the back garden, all of us shrieking. Alan and I talked late into the night, that magical time in Florida, at the gift of having such fine "boys."

Love, like God, is mystery. Why love arrives and when it does, whom it blesses and whom it curses, how it changes lives and every moment in which we breathe—all of this is beyond understanding. To love another person is to see the face of God, as Victor Hugo reminds us.

All I know is that when I am "in love," I am filled with compassion even for life's savagery, and feel forgiveness for the entire human race. Well, almost everyone.

Eli

The time in Florida is especially precious to us now, for our beloved Eli is no longer with us. Fifty-two at the time of his passing, he continues to inspire me in countless ways, and my love for him grows. Larger than life, Eli walked his days with open eyes and great perception. Though not without flaws, he was remarkably nonjudgmental and accepted people just as they were. He could talk engagingly with anyone of any age, in all countries, in secular and religious worlds. He celebrated difference. Patient and kind as a father and CEO of an internet financial reporting company, he was hugely encouraging, and helped people recognize and elevate their very best selves. Almost never rattled by life, he was the original Chasidic Taoist or Zen student. A voracious reader, he was charmingly quirky. He loved pizza reviews, and dazzling his family with esoteric knowledge and absurd questions. He was sunny-natured and naturally funny. To us, he was exceptional. I think he *was* exceptional.

Ilana, our beloved daughter-in-law, has become an outstanding photographer, and most of her photos are of people—primarily the family—engaged in life. After his death, she shared a photo of the family at the picnic celebration of Eli's last birthday. This is what you would see if you could: The entire Israeli family sits on the grass, surrounded by trees. Lots of gorgeous green. Eli is in the center of the photo. All their kids, and Eli and Ilana's grands, are dotted in circles around him.

Eli's face is lit up, his mouth open, apparently in speech. I used to tease him that he was born talking, for that kid could talk! Every single person in the photo is laughing. I have no doubt that he has just told them something quite ridiculous or has asked a patently foolish question. What you would see is joy. Joy, spirit, and playfulness were in abundance whenever Eli was present. When I am particularly sad about the loss of our son, I look at that photo on my desktop and I imagine some of what he might be saying. It could be something outrageous, as when I heard him asking our beloved grandchildren when they still lived in Toronto, in pretended seriousness, "Tell me, *kinderlach* (children), do you think it's a mistake that I married your mom?"

Brakha: Blessing

Eros awakens us to a heightened sensuality and...enables us to go beyond our individual selves.
—Lawrence Kushner, The Way into Jewish Mysticism

>It gets better
>all the time.
>
>Think wine—
>ruby burgundy
>
>shot through
>with fingers of light—
>
>a universe
>in a goblet.
>
>Where once you
>gave brief thanks,
>
>you find,
>at seventy-seven,
>
>there are no words,
>when you see
>
>him poring over
>Rhapsody in Blue,
>
>humming as he plays

the melody before

the chords.

And suddenly
you're both in there—

"boots and all,"
as they say.

He, hearing dulled
by time, and you,

who cannot type
with more than two

fingers, making music,

melodies,
and psalms,

that grab hold
of life,
and one another,

as blessings spill
into all the dusty

corners.

The Place

The place of Eros and sexuality [occur] in religious language and experience.
—Melila Hellner-Eshed, A River Flows from Eden

Your lover
moans
when you touch her
there,
sighs your name—

song
of songs.

Her eyes
open
briefly, then close
against
the flood

flash of river gold
that flows from Eden.

For this moment, you too
float
between the worlds.

Chapter 5: Encountering the Light

One Moment and the Next

Death and life are one. Together they express infinitude...
The caesura opens with both the cry of birth and the rattle of death.
—Michael Fishbane, Sacred Attunement

The days are relentless.

Nothing you can do

to prevent them from
      slipping away like a bar

of soap
    in a bubble-filled bathtub.

One moment you say yes
and your heart leaps.

The next you are staring
down your death and his,

your bodies hieroglyphs of aches
and age.

You stood, that time,

under the chuppah. Knew
you were meant to feel awe.

But all you both could do,
after exchanging stifled
laughter

and wedding rings,
was shimmer,

as you watched the rabbi's beaker

filled to the brim with blood
red
wine
      tilt dangerously

toward your white bridal gown.
So young. You both knew

you had forever.

Chapter 5: Encountering the Light

Hallelujah

The Idra says "The matter depends on love."
—Melila Hellner-Eshed, *Seekers of the Face*

Island sunset. Streaks
of red and turquoise, slashes
of gold.

The back seat is loaded—
grapes, papaya, melons,
watercress (because he loves it),
celery (because I do), carrots,
cherry tomatoes; cereal,
toilet paper,
toothpaste.

Dark chocolate, too.
With chili.
Shabbat is nigh.

Hallelujah
sings K. D. Lang,
Leonard Cohen's
poetry
stretching joyously into every
space in the little car.

I think of my body
at seventy-five, wild
with love, and the ripping

moment-to-moment awareness of each
second so precious, as Leonard,
K. D., and I sail the little bridge
over the waterway
toward home.

Shabbat is nigh. I will cart
the groceries
to our small
winter haven,
and call *help*.
And he will creak
from his computer chair,
the first few
steps somewhat bent.

"Special treat," I will say.
"Watercress.
And dark chocolate with chili."
Shabbat is nigh.

Dusk

Who knows if the blood-red dawn is the sign of birth or death in the hidden heights.
—Michael Fishbane, *Jewish Hermeneutical Theology*

There is this moment when you look
across the room at your partner

who, yawning toward eighty,
nods off, as he watches

the news. Instead

of feeling miffed,
as you
have many times, you fear

you may have to rush from the room,
folding your heart into your mouth

lest it explode into a thousand
messy sparks of love.

You and he have wandered

the corridors of marriage for more years
than Leonard Cohen spent drinking

poetry

The Light of God's Shadow

or breaking hearts. You found yourselves—
more times than you dare
remember—in the fire.

Yet this "thing"—instantly present
when you met

was just there,
and like air, could not be broken.

In this moment
inching
toward seventy-five, you discover

a little more about love, just in time to feel
your nose pressed against the mirror of mortality.

It's not that you are scared to die.

It's just that you know
life is fleeting, and love more sacred
than prayer.

So when he jerks awake, nods

at the television, smiles dreamily,
you rush from the room,

chasing

sparks of love

knowing

you're done for.

Waker-Upper

Whether we know it or not, we are in relationship all the time—with ourselves, one another, the earth, animal, and plant life, and with Ultimate Reality. Relationship, like all life, can be experienced on the manifest or hidden level. You listen to your partner's soft snoring with the occasional snort and, if you're alert to the sacred, you know you are experiencing divinity. You pause on the red brick pathway as you take out the recycling, to nod good morning to the rabbit that seems to have adopted your neighborhood, and you slip into the hidden level of creation. Any time we engage mindfully with life, even for one moment, there is the potential to wake up. You shut your eyes at the dinner table and bless your adult children, even though it's not the Sabbath. They look puzzled and pleased.

In dire need of a God fix, I leave early for my prayer-walk this morning. I stop to greet an old woman in her wheelchair and discover that Betty's stroke has left her speech intact. Her eyes sparkle with intelligence. Filled with gratitude, she says how happy she is to be able to think and speak. "It's just my right side that's gone AWOL," she reports. What a gift to be with her. Any time I give or receive friendliness, I feel bathed in God. As I continue my walk, I notice that summer has erupted early this year, and the smell of Linden blossoms makes me swoon in delight. I am surely in Eden, God-fixed for now. Thank You, Beloved.

If we are willing to look at ourselves squarely, any familial, long-term, or intimate relationship holds an especially accurate mirror to *who we are* rather than who we want to be. Waking up in relationship is a lifetime's opus and offers the possibility of making kinder choices—for ourselves, for the other, for the earth. The phone call to old Uncle Sammy, despite your dislike of him, is a spiritual act. Sharing your tomatoes and corn from the communal garden is holy. And sometimes the holy choice is not to call Uncle Sammy but to sit in the garden and do several KenKen puzzles and look for cardinals.

Consciousness, choice, and kindness are the end goals of my spiritual practices. This means I keep working to know myself as I am, to know God as God. Both are impossible, especially the God part, but the work has kept me fruitfully engaged for over forty-four years. My earliest belief was that the Holy One was all love and kindness. I keep discovering—not so much.

God inscribes our lives in a multitude of ways, including how we mess up and are "good enough" in relationships, in our minds, in our hearts. For a reflective person, there are ample opportunities for coming to consciousness as you navigate ordinary life. You notice your rudeness with the distracted person behind the counter at the gas station, then pause to pick up the fluttering sports section of the *Saturday Globe* and the empty Coke can from the sidewalk. We are called daily deeper into relationship with the radiance and darkness of life and soul, into Reality.

Single Malt Scotch

God has never been accused of not having a sense of humor.
    —Lawrence Kushner, Kabbalah: A Love Story

They had three teacups, three saucers. In a fit
of whimsy they decided
to show how each saw life.
Good china, a rose pattern.

A *mystic* and a *shaman*
they joked; sisters, seven
years apart. Much life,
for each, under well-worn
belts.

The *mystic* shut her eyes,
and with only her fingertips,
balanced teacups on saucers,
one on top of the other. Upside-
down. As above, so below.

She nodded, smiled
at her sister. The *shaman* ghosted
from the room, soon to return
with her now-adult-children's
magic markers, a huge sheet

of paper, and a damask
rose from the garden, well past
its beauty. She placed the rose

on the paper, studied it
for several minutes, then replicated

it, almost perfectly. All the while,
the *mystic* serenaded, almost inaudibly,
the rose, the teacups and saucers,
the drawing, and her sister. At the exact
moment the magic markers were placed

back into their box, signaling
the end of the exercise, Mr. Boom,
the family border collie, entered
the room. Growled, yawned,
turned counterclockwise
three times, lay down
and fell asleep.

The sisters, satisfied with the judgment
they had just received,
dismantled the demonstrations,
and in the fashion
of their departed father,
poured
themselves Scotches.
Strong.
Single Malt.

Ahava Raba—Great Love

David and I met when we were both on the Board of Spiritual Directors International. We became friends and partners in crime and have been, ever since. Still a Franciscan brother, Dave is not doing any formal "priesting" these days and has found work that makes his soul sing differently. Dave is passionate about working as a chaplain and spiritual director in a Christian eldercare home for people with cognitive disorders, Alzheimer's, and dementia, usually in the latter stages of their lives. He says that he is always learning about the Divine from companioning these people, many of whom are transparent to life. His beloved patients are on the passage to death, and their families are learning to navigate these paths with them. His patients teach him to be unadorned in the moment, with no agenda. They are present, here and now, natural, simple.

Dave is one of a handful of people with whom I do "spiritual friendship" exchanges. We have conversations in which we spend an hour together once a month. Each takes half the time to bring something for reflection, for talking and deep listening. Always sensitive and openhearted, Dave has become porous with love much of the time, and frequently moves through his days with reverence and a good sprinkling of ecstasy. He also has a healthy share of irreverence, and our meetings are punctuated by at least as much cursing and laughter as joy and wonder.

About six months ago, Dave reported an epiphany. It came at the end of a ten-day retreat. "It is simple," he said. "The world is held in love."

In our most recent conversation, Dave spoke about a remarkable experience. He was driving to work—an ordinary day—and stopped at a traffic light close to the Mississippi River in Minnesota. Suddenly the road ahead, and the homes and buildings on either side, seemed flooded in light. It was not even the river that was so wondrous, he mused. The light was not coming from outside the scene, but from inside. There was a saucer magnolia tree that was on the way out, like so many of the people David companions at work. The ground was covered in pink blossoms, fresh off the tree. "To top it off," he said, "there was a little girl dancing under the tree. She was wearing—get this—pink sneakers." It felt like he was receiving a pictorial of his epiphany: The world is held in love. He continued his drive to work and was able to feel even more love than usual for the old people he served that day, a few on the borderline of death. He, like the tableau he had witnessed, was filled with great love.

"I wish I could say it lasted," he reported, "but in a day or two, and for several days after that, I was more than usually irritable, petty, judgmental, reactive. And, damn, I could do nothing to get out of my dark state. But I thought about it, and I remembered that this, too, was God. A wholeness. The two belong together. And then I laughed with joy."

Litmus Test

One can only experience the godly through its human garb, as it arises in consciousness.
—Melila Hellner-Eshed, Seekers of the Face

The unexpected
appearance
of spirit
in my body

arrives

as tears—
a kind of visceral knowing.
Goose bumps—
behind my knees.
My breath
quickens.
    Or slows.
I salivate, for God's sake! Body
lights up,
    along the boundaries.

What causes
the *yes*
in *your* body?

For me
    a lone
star or snowflakes

fat and slow. Cardinals.
Cloud patterns
in apparent Hebrew.

A man, huge grin,
teeth
like a ragged picket fence,
ears
like conch shells.

A screaming child
who hugs
the ground. The mother
    who shrugs, crooked
smile, one eyebrow
    askew.

There is no pattern.
  I *think*
of the braiding
of light, the vibration
of sound
  and energy,
from one end
  of the universe
    to the other,
  of mystery
as my unseen
    dance partner,

the one who leads.

The Light of God's Shadow

But my body's song,
the litmus test
response
    to life,

has no relation
to *thought*.

It is the unexpected
appearance of spirit
in my body

that causes the ink
of my life to turn

from blue to gold.

River of Light

Perhaps light is, in some sense, consciousness pulsing within and unifying all being.
—Lawrence Kushner, The River of Light

Everything
suffused with light.
Several rye toast crumbs,
two sunflower seeds,
one red wine stain
on the black and white
kitchen tablecloth.
Mint, basil, rosemary, thyme
just picked from the pots
on the deck—even the aromas
seem to shine.

It's one of those days
where you could paint
with your eyes shut—
the Golden Gate
at dawn,
sunset
streaming rays
onto a freckled boy
kicking a dimpled white ball,
a lone buttercup
turned upward in greed—

one of those days

The Light of God's Shadow

where the beauty
in your eye so illumines
everything, all

you can do
is laugh.

For Larry K.

Endless Branches

God is both the source and the flow, the hidden root and the endless branches.
—Arthur Green, Seek My Face

You cannot tell me
you don't believe
in creation
as an ongoing
truth.

Just *look*
at the maples
at the end
of the garden—

their wild, ecstatic
foolishness
as leaves jitterbug
against a sailor blue
morning sky.

The skinny
branches
from which
they
    erupt

are almost
    hidden.

Then

all movement
stops

while God takes
a short break.

Like some kids
frozen
in a game
of Simon Says.

Chapter 5: Encountering the Light

The Revealed as Signpost to the Hidden

I am told by those who know things that they see only movement and light. Not only in blue herons and sunshine dancing with waves, but even in those they lunch with, and in forks and knives. Sometimes, they tell me, they almost need to shut their eyes, or spirals of light and color ablaze with energy could dazzle and overwhelm them. The only way for the rest of us to manage, may be to filter out 90 percent of our experience, and pretend the ocean we see today is the same as yesterday's. In truth, even our open-toed sandals and floppy sun hats are alive with spirit. If we do not shut tight the doors to heaven, we might fall to the ground in ecstasy, unable to walk the next step. But think about it—the miracle when, for just a moment, we allow the hidden to reveal itself, and we bend down in wonder, transfixed by the shine on the nail of our big toe.

We're All One

Animals, plants, other organisms, weather, landscape, and humans are all part of the huge, diverse ecosystem that thrives because of the Breath of Life. We are all connected to and dependent on one another. To think of this oneness is exquisite and dizzying. I haven't even mentioned planets and stars.

Soon after I was diagnosed with colon cancer, I went to the local drugstore where I receive my medications. I asked if I could speak with Evelyn, the pharmacist. We went into the tiny room off the pharmacy and she shut the door. "What's up?" she asked. "We have a good relationship," I replied. I told her I wanted her to know of my recent diagnosis and that it looked like I would be in for a long haul. "I'm inviting you onto my team," I said. Evelyn teared up. I did, too, and we hugged. After a couple of quiet moments, she told me that she was pregnant with her first child but would still be working for several months. I offered to be on her team. I told her I have three kids, fifteen grands, and a bunch of great-grands, so I knew this and that about kids. She could call me, I said. I'd probably be at home quite a bit. Birth and death. Lovely Evelyn with her first baby. And me, rubbing noses with mortality.

No one could ever have predicted what would transpire in the following six months, for, in addition to my own story of cancer, the planet was turned on its head. Most of the world went into isolation because of what people began calling the "eleventh plague." After chemotherapy and radiation in November and December of 2019, and surgery to remove my colon tumor on April 6, 2020—one day after my seventy-seventh birthday—I returned home cancer-free. No need for a colostomy of any sort. In response to COVID-19, the coronavirus that was sweeping the earth, and because of my increased vulnerability, Alan and I were in even stricter isolation than many. This was not all bad for two decided introverts.

The second day in the hospital following my surgery, I was slowly walking the corridors as instructed. One of the nurses, named Edie, pulled alongside wearing a mask—at a carefully prescribed distance. We fell into conversation. She asked about my life, if I still worked. I told her I was a spiritual director. "Tell me about your faith," she asked. I said my faith was enormously important but not in the "God will cure my cancer and prevent me from getting COVID-19" way. "Rather," I offered, "I am on the lookout for the Source of Life all the time. Since I believe that God is present in everybody and everything, I am always a student in the process of awakening—to the miracle and myriad challenges of life. And I am always asking, 'What now, my Love?' in the hope that I may receive some holy spiritual direction."

Edie's eyes shone and we began a feverish conversation, me walking at a snail's pace and Edie doing her best not to break rules by reaching across the new coronavirus divide to hug me. I told her how very grateful I am to be free of cancer and sans a colostomy. I said that I have been Reiki-ing myself and visualizing shrinking the tumor for months. "I have no idea if it helped," I told Edie, "but I know it did not hurt." Edie became all hushed and confidential and said she believes patients have a hand in their own healing. "I also think God is part of every single person," she whispered. Her faith in something larger positively bounced off her. Just walking together, at the safe distance, reminded me that Evelyn, Edie, and I are simply different faces of the One. Our words are just what we speak to give us something to do while we are holding soul-hands.

CHAPTER 6: REDISCOVERING THAT I'M INCURABLY HUMAN

Are You Still Here?

In a timeless or spaceless dimension, death is not a complete or final annihilation.
—Melila Hellner-Eshed, *Seekers of the Face*

For my son Eli, August 1968–November 2020

I do not want
to hear
how your soul will live
on—in Chasky's quirky
humor, Tully's dazzling
smile, Ruchie's designs,
Elky's Buddhist ease.

I do not want
to know
how you still inspire
countless—including
your mother—
to be better
than we are.

What I want to do
is send another "Call your mother"
email, learn what you are

reading—Dostoevsky? The Dalai Lama?
You were always such a catholic
Jew.

I want to be
in your kitchen
before Shabbos—
Ilana making challah,
you, Israeli couscous,
and hummus—with your secret
ingredient—as you deliver
one of your Eli-zingers:
"Tell the truth
kinderlach, do you think
that Moishe looks more like me,
or like Curious George?"

Chapter 6: Rediscovering That I'm Incurably Human

A Big, Fat "I Don't Know"

I've seen him around a lot. Often when I drop into Metro for a last-minute top-up of tomatoes or milk. A couple or more teeth are missing from his lower jaw. Just the top button of his shirt closes, straining gallantly. He's made Lawrence Plaza his home from what I can tell. Always drinks Diet Coke.

I approach him one day. Offer him a few bucks. Lady Bountiful. "No, thank you," he says, looking long at me. "But know what? You can say hello when you see me next time. Oh, and God bless you. Truly, God bless you."

It wasn't in my plans to have a relationship with him, but rather to graciously drop some money his way from time to time. I see him about ten days later, Diet Coke in hand, sitting in the sun outside Second Cup, where those with time linger over lattes, frappes, or whatever they're calling coffees these days.

I stop. "Hello." His face crinkles in recognition. This time I look long at him. He is "home," very present behind the surprisingly blue, surprisingly youthful eyes.

"Beautiful day," he says. It is. One of those late fall days when you keep saying, "Thank You" to the Source of Life. We talk about the weather a bit. Climate change. He shakes his head at how we humans have messed up.

"What's your name?" I ask.

"Bobby."

"Hi Bobby. I'm Jinks." I bow like a Buddha, a bit remorseful that I'm not yet ready to extend both hands in greeting. He suggests that the next time we meet, the weather may not be as good. The next time? We have a future now.

This God stuff—I can't decide where I stand. Bobby holds a mirror to my privilege and judgment. Sometimes doors close, and from the ashes of terrible crises new life can emerge. My colon cancer seems to have kicked the hell out of my overfocus on my health. For now. My time of dread has taught me more about not having control than I imagined possible. I do not believe that God gave me cancer or that God makes Bobby's life difficult and mine mainly a blessing. Am I even correct in assuming that Bobby's life is difficult? Is the Holy One initiating this reverie about Bobby? I don't know. Why does Bobby, patently impoverished, sit in public if he doesn't want money? I don't know. Is Bobby God, trying to wake me up more to the divine spark in all humans? Is my somersault of consciousness—of awakening to my small-mindedness—of any value? I don't know that, either. I do believe that every moment of life offers potential learning, and my life is one big, fat "I don't know." I like to imagine, though, that God is present and Bobby is teaching me something about holiness—also that God is grinning!

Love in the Time of COVID-19

The rush of Mystery frightens in the first summer of COVID-19. Nasty winds whip our hair into knots as we walk in our neighborhood. There is nothing but uncertainty at which to grasp. Careful to keep the requisite six-foot distance from others, we encounter something unusual. Usually reserved Canadians call out warm though slightly woeful greetings to one another, and offer words of encouragement. Family members and friends connect more frequently—online or by phone. The tenor of the day seems to be "What can I do to help?"

Many are reflecting on this time in our lives as a call from the Universe to wake up. I read an online admonition that asked, "Do you ever feel that God has sent us to our rooms to think about what we have done?" Some posit that the Divine became desperate at our lack of love for the earth, for one another, for ourselves, and thus brought us to our knees. Others explain this devastating time scientifically. There are conspiracy theories. Much is being said and written in this time out of time. Everyone has their own story, their own viewpoint, their own banner to wave. I don't *know* anything, but I have a sense that we are being called to slow down and listen more—to the heartbeat of the earth, to one another, and to however we frame the sacredness of life. I know that I don't want to go back to "normal" when the pandemic is over. "Normal" before the pandemic moved a little too fast and a little too noisily for me.

I don't know how to think about God and COVID-19, though I suspect that I have been invited to row to yet another island, to plant more seeds of uncertainty and unknowing. I frequently feel sorrow and anxiety—for my family and myself. Even more, for all of humanity. We are living through a time unlike anything we have known. Along with my uncertainty and sorrow, I am grateful to feel love every day—for cherry tomatoes that keep arriving on the plants on the deck. For Ilana, our daughter-in-law, who frequently posts extraordinary photographs of their large brood of kids, studies in light and dark, sunlight catching tendrils of the twins' hair, their long, blue dresses in shadow.

One day recently, feeling particularly miserable, I came upstairs for my Zoom conversation with Tully. Tully, at twenty-seven, is one of our six grandsons and we meet monthly to have spiritual conversations. He, with his bright eyes and infectious smile, spoke of all the spiritual reading he is doing, of how he is realizing, more all the time that waking up is not a once-and-for-all phenomenon. I experienced God-tears and God goose bumps, I told him. This is a time on earth when we meet—maybe more than usual—the complexity of God. This is the Divine I cannot know, and yet I do, as my heart and body feel wonder and tremble. This is my God. This is love.

A Dream and a Legend as Consciousness Raisers

When my beloved mother was dying of pancreatic cancer in 1995, I had a dream that told me: *I ask questions and God buzzes in*. Daily visits to the palliative care unit of Baycrest Hospital were proving heartbreaking. Once so vibrant and full of spirit, Mom had become shrunken and gaunt, frequently in a restless sleep. I sat beside her bed day after day, praying for her comfort and peace. Even when a person is in a coma, many believe that souls know when others are with them. I wished so much that my tuneless lullabies could soothe my mother's restlessness. And then I remembered that dream. "Hey, God," I prayed, "what do I do here? Please buzz in. I do not believe You gave my mother cancer. Can You, though, please help me feel Your love as I behold my mother's dying? And even more importantly, can You ease her passage?"

Sometimes when I pray, a thought arrives that has a distinctly "other" feel to it. It seemed that I received some guidance those many years ago that was so powerful I remember the gist of it today. "Do your best to flow with what life brings to you. Know that while you are responsible for a great deal, you control very little. Surrender to Me. Work like the devil. Then give it up. I'm the boss." And then, as I recall, God reminded me of the principles of Taoism: simplicity, patience, compassion, and going with the flow. It seems that the Holy One is pretty inclusive, and frankly, I think, was showing off. These words are my compass. I am still a beginner at surrender.

Chapter 6: Rediscovering That I'm Incurably Human

I had a dream once: *Tonight, you meet the Baal Shem Tov.* There is a legend about the Baal Shem Tov ("Master of the Great Name"), a Jewish mystic and healer and the founder of Chasidic Judaism. He was walking in the woods one winter day when he beheld an old woman in rags dragging a sled on which sat a little boy, also dressed in rags. Witnessing these two poor, miserable, cold, and hungry beings, he cried out, "God, God, how can you permit such misery in the world? How can you behold these poor creatures and do nothing? The widow and the orphan. Do something, please." There was no answer. Again, the Baal Shem Tov cried out, "God, please answer me. How is it possible for you to behold such misery and do nothing about it?" Again, no answer, just wind in the treetops. The Baal Shem Tov cried out once again, "Holy One, I beg of you, answer me." At last came an answer in the heart of the Master of the Great Name: "I did do something. I created you."

We are God's hands in the world. While responsible for a great deal, we control very little. There are infinite ways we can be God's hands in the world, like easing the suffering of others, tending the poor and marginalized, spreading love in action.

Again

> Shekhinah roams the...world, and it is there among the
> people...that she finds a place to reside.
> —Melila Hellner-Eshed, A River Flows from Eden

You're sitting at the dinner table. It is late,
the eyes of the night heavy. Plates
and pots need washing, the stovetop simulating

a Jackson Pollock piece.
Your sweetheart scrapes, with the heel
of a crusty baguette,
the last of the puttanesca.

And then, it happens.
Again. You're Moses, and the bush
is burning. Your belly floods

with a heat that beats from the middle,

stretching all the way to the limits
of your limbs, fingertips, and tingling toes,

skin a rise of goose bumps saying yes.

How can you know when the Beloved
will make herself known? How can you know

why Shekhinah has come to sit with you,
to share your good fortune and bless you? Is it

Chapter 6: Rediscovering That I'm Incurably Human

because

you allowed him the last lengths of linguine,
the last sop of sauce? Maybe it's because you
intend to do the washing up. Stovetop and all.

But you cannot know. Ever. Or *make* it happen.
All you can do, is whisper *yes*, and bless *him*,
the goose bumps, and the heat in your body,

which moves and loves you, all the way
through, till it joins the river
that flows from the Garden of Eden.

An Apple a Day

On the eighth day of the eighth month of 1988, I went into the hospital to have a small lump removed from my left breast. There was cancer in that small lump. I am a recovering hypochondriac, and on that memorable day of all eights, my lifelong journey into developing a conscious relationship with life and death received quite the jolt. A few months post-surgery, I went to see my surgeon for a follow-up visit. He told me that although there had been no cancer in my lymph nodes, research suggested chemotherapy for all people with even well-contained breast cancer. With great apprehension, I made appointments to see two oncologists. Like Asclepius going into the temple for guidance, I asked my dreams to talk to me. Soon after, I had two dreams. One simply said, *an apple a day*, and the other comfortingly told me, *You don't need it. You will live into your eighties.*

It was an anxious time until I visited the oncologists. My dreams had nixed chemotherapy. What would I do if I were advised to have chemotherapy—listen to the doctors, or to what I believed to be God talking though my dreams? At the time of my first cancer, I was forty-five. "Into my eighties" seemed to be an eternity away. Now, at seventy-eight, not so much. Happily, both oncologists agreed with my dreams, so I didn't have to choose. I like to think I would have chosen the Divine.

My dream *an apple a day* led me to reflect on Eden. Adam and Eve ate an apple from the Tree of Knowledge of Good and Evil although they were forbidden to do so. They were expelled from the Holy Garden. Some teachers of Jewish mysticism believe that before birth, the soul is with God in a state of wholeness. Once born, we are expelled from paradise because we have split

Chapter 6: Rediscovering That I'm Incurably Human

good and evil, rather than recognizing that both exist in life and in our psyche. The lifelong journey back to Eden—or to union with the Beloved—involves becoming familiar with and accepting evil, the shadow darkness in our souls, in humanity, and also in the Holy One. This is the process of becoming conscious of the totality of who we are, rather than who we would like to be or were socialized to be. If we do this, there is less chance that we will act violently or with cruelty. Many mass murderers are deeply traumatized children at heart, whose pain and suffering have been buried in their unconscious.

    Now, at seventy-eight, I reflect on surviving cancer again, this time colon cancer. What am I to learn from the Tree of Life and the Tree of Knowledge of Good and Evil this time? Can I live with even deeper authenticity, open even more to the light and the darkness? Can I immerse myself in the moment just as it is? Can I stay with my pain—whatever it is—until it is done—for this now? I go for my morning prayer-walk full of sorrow. I grieve about the challenges the colon cancer has left in my body, about our beloved Eli being gone forever. I feel sorrow for all the trouble the world is in, for the surfacing of the new Delta variant in the pandemic. I pray that people will be double vaccinated in time to prevent yet more tragic deaths. I whisper to the Beloved—I often talk as I walk—that I am sorry to be so sad when the day is shining with early summer green and new roses in exuberant bloom. I say that I wish I weren't so sensitive, that I didn't feel sad so often. And then I hear my thoughts telling me lovingly not to be an idiot. I am me—sensitive, and richly sad and joyous. God wants us to be ourselves, and even more so. And then my heart begins to sing with the scent of the Japanese lilac trees that have started to flower all over the neighborhood. I decide that, for this moment anyway, I will live mindfully with the full catastrophe, as Jon Kabat-Zinn invites us to do. Now I stop to talk with a woman who obviously puts hours of work into her glorious garden. We are still COVID-distanced, but I can easily send across the road my appreciation for the beauty she creates. That's how it is for me. When I hold my own wobbly feelings with tenderness, what happens almost instantly is a flowering of my caring, concern, and often love for others.

Prayer

I pray a lot. Mostly, when I do, I listen for those thoughts and emotions that feel other than mine. Maybe I am intuiting the Beloved? I think of prayer as energy directed toward the pray-ee. My friend's husband is dying. She says she has pared down her life to the essential. Love is essential, she says. Also rubbing his dear wasted back. I tell her I pray for healing for both and hasten to explain that I don't mean cure. My friend is Buddhist. My prayers feel like one seed of a grape tomato when what is needed is a whole baked salmon, fresh bread, salad, and rice. And wine. I pray "Thank you" for my friend, her hours of rubbing, changing bed linens, learning ever more about patience. Also, for her wicked sense of humor—especially her jokes about death. Wiser folks than I seem confident about knowing the big stuff, knowing God. I just pray a lot. Makes my belly feel good. Maybe, though, sometimes what is needed is prayer-in-action—salmon, bread, salad, and rice. Oh, and wine.

Suffering One and Suffering Two: A Perspective

We're in the soup from time to time. Pretending to ourselves that we're not just makes it worse. There is no way to get out of the soup permanently until we die. And even then, who knows? In the children's book *The Cat in the Hat* by Dr. Seuss, we meet Thing One and Thing Two. They are not exemplars of exquisite order. Let out of a box, they fly a kite in the house that bumps into walls and causes all sorts of mayhem. Perhaps we can differentiate between Suffering One and Suffering Two. Who doesn't suffer? Suffering One issues from our place of wholeness and alignment with Reality—the Divine. We suffer when our aging bodies struggle with simple skills that were once easy, when we see whole neighborhoods on fire. We suffer when our babies have colic and cry inconsolably, when our children die at fifty-two. Parents are not supposed to live longer than their children. This is Suffering One.

Suffering Two shows up from our tender, messed-up place. We unconsciously create suffering to avoid Suffering One, when what we actually need and long for is witness and compassion—from another, from ourselves. Tears beg witness. To hold our own anguish with compassion may be one of our most important spiritual tasks. I cannot say this enough. No part of us should be stuffed into a box and banished. Knowing all of who we are, accepting all the bits, and then lovingly containing the destructive aspects of our psyche is the goal. To put it another way, a combo of lovingkindness and firmness—or *chesed* and *gevurah* as we might say in Jewish mysticism.

Bea worked with me in psychotherapy many years ago. She fretted about the big and small potatoes of her life. When she lay down to sleep at night, she worried for a long time about things that never happened: Would she be late for work if the subway system broke down again? It had, two weeks ago. Would her boss ask her to stay late? Was the egg salad still fresh? It smelled fine, but she'd had it for five days already. Bea and I spent years working with her dreams, paying attention to her relationship challenges, and noticing the synchronicities in her life. Bea also began to become aware that she resisted feeling her emotions. "I fret a lot," she said, "but otherwise, I am pretty numb." When Bea learned gradually to allow herself to feel fear and vulnerability that was fully alive, she began to vividly remember painful times in her childhood, in her family of origin. Her mother had been a drug user with erratic periods of abstinence. Her father was a retired judge who had little patience or humor. There was not much softness in the home, little attention paid to a sensitive child. For Bea as an adult, when she lay down to sleep, it was easier to worry about egg salad than to remember the pain, loneliness, and fear she felt as a little girl. For Bea as an adult, Suffering Two was trumping Suffering One and keeping her imprisoned in her mind. As Bea learned to go in and down, to inhabit her body and emotions, she became more able to stay with her sorrow and fear. Over time she became more able to parent the child within her, the child still longing to be the loving center of someone's heart.

Because COVID-19 had changed the world and our lives, I went alone into the hospital for my surgery to remove cancer from my colon. Alan collected me three days later outside the front doors of the hospital. Once home, I wept at times about this trauma and pain. This was Suffering One—simple and pure pain, uncontaminated by any of my blessed neuroses. My Suffering Two complex could have spent countless obsessive hours fretting about whether the cancer was completely gone and whether it will recur in the future. I surely know Suffering Two, and part of my awakening is to recognize when he's inveigling his way into my consciousness.

Chapter 6: Rediscovering That I'm Incurably Human

The Buddhists, I learned, talked about Suffering One and Suffering Two long before I discovered them. They call the teaching the Second Arrow. We get pierced by life's arrows at times. That hurts. Ow! First arrow. Then we say nasty things to ourselves about the pain of the first arrow, like, "Stop being such a neurotic baby." Second arrow.

Eden, Differently

The dew drips continuously...bit by bit...this light, this life force...into the Orchard of Holy Apples.
—Melila Hellner-Eshed, Seekers of the Face

Apples almost burst with the shine
of red and white lovemaking.
Bees, in their ecstasy
disturb the luscious air.
The smell of earth
dazzles.

The Holy Apples are ready
to drop, just like orbs
of dew glistening
in sunlight.
The hum
of the universe
is audible only
if you stand still
for a long time.

Now

   turn around

      count
       your
        steps
         forward

   and walk
      under
the lattice of vines
heavy with grapes
into the Orchard.

This Is Real and You Are Completely Unprepared

(Trying to stay) morally awake in a world rife with terror.
—Tirzah Firestone, Wounds into Wisdom

A door slams.
My life as I knew it
is over. I stand
between this place
and that, not knowing
what I will find
when that door opens. I only know
I cannot open it
myself.
I have no words, only a heart
that often thuds
in terror, yet
in this blessed moment
soars
with joy
for the gift of life.
I have learned

something
in my years.
If I stand steady
in this place of not-knowing,
feet a bit apart,
and do not cling—desperate
for safety—to anything,
my hands are free

to pluck
coins from the ears
of children, do a creaky
cartwheel, and rub the belly
of the Rottweiler who lies
suddenly before me,
paws aloft
in surrender.

Source: Adapted from Alan Lew, *This Is Real and You Are Completely Unprepared: The Days of Awe as a Journey of Transformation* (New York: Back Bay Books, 2018).

What or Where Is God?

Our seven-year-old granddaughter had a sleepover with us last night. This morning we are eating breakfast together. Ayla, bless her, asks a lot of questions. "Where is God, Bubby?" The seductress.

"Tell me first what *you* think, Ayla."

Without hesitation, she says, "God is everywhere."

I nod enthusiastically. "I agree."

Ayla pauses thoughtfully and points to her breakfast. "Not the blueberries or milk or glass," she offers. "Just the air."

"W-e-l-l," I answer, "maybe God is everywhere *and* everything. After all, I think blueberries were created by God, and cows also."

"Not the glass." Ayla is bossy, like her Bubby.

"Maybe that, too." I pantomime a large inclusive dance, arms ballerina-wide, trying to seduce Ayla right back. "After all, glass was initially made by a person."

"What's *initially* mean?" Ayla asks, and we're on a roll. But a few moments later she ends the conversation.

"We don't know what God is," she says authoritatively.

Our seven-year-old mystic. I'm with Ayla.

We cannot *know*—with certainty—anything about the Holy One of All Being. There are grandchildren with blue eyes and tenderhearted friends who celebrate small victories with us. There are tornadoes, the new coronavirus, and political arenas in certain countries in the world that are terrifying and chaotic. There are pogroms and cures for polio. The whole damn enterprise appears at times to be completely arbitrary and uncontrollable. And I keep learning that the primary purpose behind it all is the love, curiosity, and hunger of the Divine to keep creating and getting to know Godself.

Who* Is Crying

God has a hidden life within the mind of man, but actual thinking can only occur within the framework of the human mind.
—Sanford Drob, Kabbalistic Visions: C. G. Jung and Jewish Mysticism

So here we are, on the old pine chair,
faded red cushions, grumpy
fall morning.
We want only birdsong,
not the children
fighting,
and father shadowboxing
in the yard
next door.

I wonder how it is
for You,
with me, here,
in this body
of seventy-five
as I scribble
feverish words—

my hopeful attempt
to give shape
to the knowing

it is not really me

    thinking
        scribbling,
           listening
                to the call
of a courting cardinal
but You,

who
    listens
        scribbles
           thinks

now
prays
tears streaming
down.

Why do You-in-my-body-thinking-it's-me
cry with joy, every time
that veil

      just for an instant
                        drops away?

*In mystical Judaism, Who is one of God's names.

Who is Crying (Reprise)

The very significance of divine thought is contingent upon this thought making its appearance in the mind of man.
—Sanford Drob, Jung, Kirsch, and Judaism.

So here we are, on the old pine chair
cushions gentled
by time, by air,
in our winter
haven,
which feels
anything
but healing.

My belly hurts,
  fingertips
    and toes
      numb
        from chemotherapy.
          The burns
            from the radiation
              ache and itch.

I am scared.

My breath
  slows—in
      then out;
  I pray
    I weep

I wonder—
how it is for You,
        in this seventy-seven-year-old body
which mirrors
the blue
of this winter morning.

Then I remember
Who
breathes.

CHAPTER 7: WAKING UP AGAIN AND AGAIN

And Then...

That special openness of the soul...standing in silent witness...
—Arthur Green, *Judaism for the World*

I notice a small branch
on Fairlawn Avenue.
Tiny, bare, a Tai Chi pose,
it lies vulnerable
in the busy road.
I bring it home, place
it in a single bud vase.
Slowly pour
water in.

For just a few moments
I stand guard every day
over this offering
and witness
as the end
of each tiny offshoot
morphs
into a bud,
and then

blooms.

It's like being

a friend
to this small branch,
my reverent daily attention
teaching the thing its loveliness,
until,
as Galway Kinnell once said,
it blossoms from within,
of self-blessing.

Chapter 7: Waking Up Again and Again

The One Who Reads These Words

To realize that right now, at this very moment, the one who reads these words is being created by God, is to...enter the mystical Nothingness of God.
—Lawrence Kushner, The Way into the Jewish Mystical Tradition

The one who reads
these words

could be Carl Jung

who dreams
he is a butterfly,

or a butterfly
who dreams

he is Carl Jung—

especially if the one who reads
knows
past   present   future
exist
all at once.

If, however, *you* feel
a soprano-like shiver

up your very spine

The Light of God's Shadow

    as your eyes ghost

    from one word
    to the next,
    it is possible, God,

    it is You who reads.

Chapter 7: Waking Up Again and Again

Just Everything Slowing

How can we possibly realize that the bush is burning without being consumed unless we linger? Mystery may only reveal itself if we look long enough, if we listen. We suspect that the world, inside and out, is on fire with divinity but we cannot know this if we slipstream our days. I have had a few blessed brushes with Mystery, so early this morning I sit, wild with longing. I flutter my eyes closed—butterfly wings. Brush my cheeks with fingertips. I can sometimes, I swear, feel the breath of God right here. I sit a long while.

There is construction nearby. A saw whines on and off, ending with a petulant whistle. I am tired, despite ample sleep. Squirrels chase one another irritably up and down the Norway maples at the end of the garden. Time passes. My *tuches* hurts. How long have I been sitting? I am so not the ideal sitting meditator. Where is the promised Eden in this moment?

I flutter my eyes shut again. Listen, in and out. Once, twice, three times. Nothing.

And then...there is a lushness. I can sense it. A tear descends my cheek, my breath begins a soft humming. Everything slows. No miracles. No rainbows and marching bands. No angels or hallelujahs. Just a lushness. And everything slowing.

Both/And

Goldie thought she might be suicidal. Although she was seeing a psychiatrist, Goldie decided she also wanted companioning from a spiritual director. After twelve years of deep work, Goldie said that while she liked sitting in spiritual direction, she felt ready to end our sessions. No longer suicidal, and much better able to manage the darkness, Goldie had learned that there is no cure for the deep sorrow that comes and goes. She declared that by sitting in reflection in our sessions and listening to her deepest wisdom, she had received two invaluable gifts: compassion for her suffering and the perspective of both/and. When depressed, she told me in one of our final sessions, she lay on her bed and allowed her tears. She placed one hand on her belly, stroked her heart with the other, and imagined that she was a great, big mama, murmuring, "Ai-yai-yai, it's OK, Baby."

Life is both/and. Daily there is wonder—a male cardinal resting briefly next to the sunshine-yellow begonias on the railing of the deck. Two men sitting on the back of their flatbed truck, looking in opposite directions, and roaring with laughter. A tenderhearted mother saying to her adult daughter, "What else? Tell me everything." And in 2020 and 2021, in the dark and repeated waves of the new eleventh plague in the world, there is untold suffering. People die alone in hospitals and nursing homes. Proud families without money or resources, terrified of being evicted from their homes, have no choice but to turn to food banks. Moms or dads who work full time on the front lines return to cranky children who have been cooped up indoors all day. We celebrate with men on trucks laughing in comradeship, and we ache for family members who cannot comfort one another around the graveside of their kin—frontline workers who died of COVID-19.

With her integration of the wisdom of both/and, and her practice of self-compassion, Goldie had come to a place in her psyche that is a game changer. Perhaps we don't need much more than this, any of us—to know that light and dark both belong in the totality of who we are. And to have tenderness for "incurable humanity"—our own and that of our fellow travelers.

Chapter 7: Waking Up Again and Again

Goldie said that at times the darkness was unremitting: No matter how hard she worked by reading spiritual texts, meditating, reflecting on dreams, journaling, exercising, eating well, being kind to herself and others—nothing shifted her pain. At other times she awakened in good spirits that lasted the whole day. "Darkness is darkness," she said. "It has a mind of its own." No one can ever know what it is like to live inside another's soul. "Darkness is darkness," I agreed quietly.

I confessed to Goldie that my desire to help lift her despair occasionally came not only from my deep caring for her but also from my desire to "save" her. She smiled at my *shmutz* cleaning. Our job is not to fix anybody but to attend reverently to their souls.

"I don't need saving," Goldie said.

My teacher.

Change Is the Only Constant

I went to see my Jungian analyst just after a particularly challenging period in my life, when my psyche had been what in Yiddish we call *vermisht*— "messed up." I secretly thought I was almost there—wholeness and complete unity with God a mere breath away. Bob listened intently. When I had finished my triumphant recounting of dreams and the raw material of my life, he did not leap up and pump my hand in a congratulatory manner but simply said, "Yes."

Barely hiding my disappointment, I asked if I have simply been rediscovering the wheel all my many years of analysis. Bob smiled kindly. "Those of us in the consciousness game keep working on the same material. But if we stay close to the bone, we may spiral down and get quicker at catching the complexes when they appear. Closer to center," he said. He told me about one of his favorite cartoons in the *New Yorker*. The scene is of two men. One older. It is clear from the picture that the young man is the devil. He is saying to the older man "Can I come in?" The older man struggles discernibly and then says, "Yes." The devil turns to the viewer, grins and says, "All I need is a small opening. Only a small opening."

Bob said that through our work we keep narrowing that opening, for without consciousness, the devil—or the ways our particular wounds or dark archetypal energies manifest—can move in, suitcase in hand, and take residence in our heads. Consciousness of habitual patterns and feeling the pain, anger, and confusion in the dark places, make it harder for the devil to slip in. This is an important aspect of our psychospiritual work and helps us find compassion for ourselves and others. If we can accept ourselves most deeply, our relationships get better. Jungian psychology, Buddhism, and Kabbalah tell us that we cannot control life. The ground of our existence is always in movement, and change is the only constant. Learning to live in free fall may be the goal of deep work. And while we fall, please may we notice the proverbial wild strawberry in the cleft in the rock. Amen.

Becoming older and more conscious may also help us know that we're not in control. I confess that I still think I have found the magic bullet every time I squeak through a period of darkness or when my *shmutz* no longer runs rampant. But though I am not cured, it seems that the devil stays for shorter and shorter periods. This, then, may be success in therapy: greater consciousness of our messy parts and the ability to show them the door more quickly. It helps, too, if we befriend our wounded places, develop compassion for them, and get to know them in every nook and cranny.

Sadie and Others: Creativity as a Means of Survival

Creative people often feel more engaged, more content, more joyful. Creativity is also a good way to ward off our personal demons. Mike is a lawyer in a large company and has three young sons. Life is busy and stressful for him and his doctor wife. He sought spiritual direction because of a vague ennui. While his physical health was good, his soul was not. In our time together, Mike spoke intermittently of a longing he'd had since childhood to write a book. When he mentioned his dream, his voice softened and his usually tense shoulders dropped slightly. I wondered if he was possibly hearing from his soul. "Maybe," he said, "but this will have to wait until the boys are older." I suggested that he read Julia Cameron's *The Artist's Way* and recommended that he begin with the Morning Pages—longhand, stream-of-consciousness writing done first thing in the morning. "Writers need to write," I said. At first he demurred, but after a while Mike began rising an hour before everyone in the family to write reflectively. After several months he told me that he had not missed one day of writing. "Cameron speaks of God," he said. "I don't know what God is, but no matter how stressful today is, I think to myself that I will have tomorrow morning's writing to help me work with my stress and live my life a little more easily." Mike has not yet found his book, but he has found the thread to his own soul. I mentioned slyly that some people write even more than once a day. Afternoon, or evening pages, I said. Mike looked sideways at me: "Hmmm," he said.

In her book, Cameron writes about living creatively as a way of enhancing spiritual life. She does not limit creativity to making art, such as writing, painting, or sculpting, for example. She believes, as did Carl Jung, that perhaps the greatest artist is one who lives with a fullness of spirit and vitality, with a connection to the unconscious. She believes that the Great Creator, whom she unabashedly calls God, loves engagement in any form and actively helps those who open themselves to their creativity. When we attend to our creative spirit, we are a conduit for the Great Artist to express and expand its divine nature.

Nora and I have worked together for seven years. She is a successful artist. She believes her work has become stale, that she is producing the same paintings in varying disguises. She knows she is avoiding entering the dark and mysterious place in her psyche, that she needs to "go in" to the place of not-knowing. She understands that she may feel chaos, anxiety, maybe pain. She fears the emptiness. Who doesn't? "What if there's nothing there?" she asks. It is from the emptiness—the fertile void—that new birth may be created. Many run in place or discover addictions that compel to ward off the abyss. Nora cripples herself by thinking about the art she will produce should she enter the darkness that looms. What if people no longer like her work? What if she can no longer be successful? These are all good questions, yet unless Nora goes into her room and enters the void, she will likely be stuck—less than her fullest self.

Most of us find ourselves facing the seemingly daunting unknown at least a few times in our lives. This may be because we have suffered illness or loss or, as in 2020 and 2021, because we are living in dark and frightening times over which we have little control. Studying how our wounds currently appear in our lives and befriending them can be dramatically healing. Few choose to enter a place of chaos voluntarily. If we do, we will

Chapter 7: Waking Up Again and Again

be required to surrender a certain level of real or imaginary control over our lives. This can be terrifying. But if we stay in our bodies and become deeply attentive to our hearts and the mix of feelings we have, we may learn something. Especially if we can hold all our painful, vulnerable feelings tenderly.

I had a wonderful visit with my friend Lucinda Hage recently. We talked for a good long time about her book *What Time Is the 9:20 Bus? A Journey to a Meaningful Life, Disability and All*, which is about Lucinda's son, Paul. She adopted him as a baby. Soon after, she discovered he had tuberous sclerosis complex, a serious illness that caused baby Paul to have seizures. He subsequently developed an intellectual disability. Over a long and painful period, Paul also began to exhibit severe behavioral and emotional disorders. Lucinda's book is about how she worked to ensure that her son would have as many opportunities in life as possible, be as independent as he could be, and become a functioning member of society. Lucinda wrote the book for her soul's sake. Also, because she learned so much through raising her son, she wanted to share what is possible.

My husband Alan receives invitations from the deep from time to time, inspiration to begin some new activity. Ten years ago, he began playing the piano again, and has become somewhat nimble with a tune. I name the deep "God"; Alan doesn't give it a name. His latest call, coinciding somewhat with my colon cancer, was to begin sewing. He bought a modest Brother sewing machine and got to work. I teasingly call him Sadie Seamstress. For eighteen months he has been making a variety of women's bags, totes, and backpacks of all descriptions, in many dazzling and contrasting colors. All the Canadian and Israeli females in the family—and there are many—are proud owners of a Sadie-special. I have four. An accountant and then a businessman until he retired, Alan has always been meticulous about time. Now he loses himself for hours in the act of creation. I pass his office and hear the happy whirring of Brother.

Brian is a former graphic designer and successful businessman. He retired and became an artist and teacher. He talked once with Alan and me about teaching his students to draw portraits of live models in no more than fifteen minutes. All Brian's creations sold in short order. "Only fifteen minutes," we remarked in wonder, "and your portraits are fantastic."

"Thirty years and fifteen minutes," Brian replied.

Down to the Bone

The twin needs—for quiet and self-protection and telling and connection—have to be honored.
—Tirzah Firestone, Wounds into Wisdom

All but the conifers are bare now—skeleton
trees sentinel on my daily drive. Everything
reduced to its essence: no verdant grasses,
poppies
or lilacs, a gloom of monotone
sky, and the few stragglers walking dogs
on icy sidewalks. The Honda hums tunelessly
as I crank up the heat on my way
to the hospital. These winter days I am
pared of all I am used to.

I've learned

to manage the preparation—
several slow sips of water until I am ready
for the radiation that will soon be poured
into my weary body.

    I have come to like the small
retreats into muffled quiet: the drive to the hospital,
returning to our softer home, the open spaces
in my days. Time does what it does
when you pay attention, the slow
and the still
pointing to moments

The Light of God's Shadow

of translucency—despite
this dark winter
of my life. "You must be counting
the days," people say, "till the chemo and radiation
are over." I smile. I am not counting anything,
my suffering having shot me through
into the here and the now.
                      Hollowed
out by tenderness I think of the others
in the Cancer Center—the trembling
hands, hairless heads, haunted eyes.

"Visualize white light," they say,
"destroying
your tumor."
I smile, having no need to visualize
anything.
I see a woman wearing a hijab.
She pushes an empty stroller, while her tiny
girl,
wearing a white angora sweater and harlequin
tights totters unsteadily behind her.
"Good walking," I say. The girl smiles.
The mother
shines and replies, "She's eighteen
months."

                    I think
of the Hebrew symbol for eighteen:
chai, which means life.
"She was born

all bone," the mother says, "two months preemie, at this hospital."

"And now, she's perfect."

John at JCPenney

> *The paradox of loving seems to be that you get bigger by making yourself smaller.*
> —Lawrence Kushner, God was in this Place & I, i did not know

He's been advising customers
for twenty years, he tells—fitting,
measuring, checking
prescriptions.
Took several courses
to improve.
Knows
eyes and glasses
like the back
of his hand, he says,
turning his head to the left
then the right to ensure
the glasses sit perfectly
on her small nose. Is careful
not to touch her face.
Gives
a small nod of satisfaction,
an almost audible grunt.

His father was a carpenter, he says.
His mother a teacher of special
needs kids. Hard work,
he says, runs in the family.
Pats his belly. I'm Chatty
Cathy, he smiles,

and reddens a little,
almost becomingly.

Learning and Teaching

Our good friend Lin went into the hospital for a small and routine mitral valve repair when she was seventy. During the operation, a tear in her aorta was discovered. Several crises occurred during the surgery, and we will never know whether the tear was caused by the procedure or by some flaw that had existed previously. Lin spent ten hours on the operating table. During this time, blood and oxygen did not reach her legs and feet. Not too many survive such trauma.

Lin nearly died. Her life hung in the balance for several weeks. She was in the hospital for three months, during which time it became apparent that if she were to live, she would have to have her legs amputated from above her knees. She would never walk again. Prosthetics were not an option. Lin spent several days choosing between life and death. If she opted not to have the double amputation, the sepsis would surely kill her.

Lin's and my friendship dates to South African days before we were both married. From the early days of our connection, we have shared a sense of being rooted in the Divine and both reverence and irreverence about life. Perhaps they're the same thing. In the dark, surreal period of time when Lin was choosing between life and death, we talked and prayed and asked her dreams for guidance. Lin's family—a loving husband and three wonderful children—held the ground while she decided. There were times when it looked like she would choose death. She did not.

In the Lakota-Sioux tradition, a person who is grieving is considered most holy. There's a sense that when someone is struck by the sudden lightning of loss, he or she stands on the threshold of the spirit world. You might recall what it's like to

Chapter 7: Waking Up Again and Again

be with someone who has grieved deeply. The person has no layer of protection, nothing left to defend. Mystery is looking out through that person's eyes. In the groundless openness of sorrow, a wholeness of presence and a deep natural wisdom suffuse our being.

Lin spent three months in a rehabilitation hospital where she received help in gaining body strength, learning to live with her new body, becoming more independent. After this, she returned to their home, which had been renovated to accommodate her changed body.

Five years later, Lin has learned to be in this new life in a way that inspires. She has many friends who continue to visit, to play bridge and Scrabble. To schmooze. She hosts a Torah study class at her home on Wednesdays. She and her husband, Alan, share Shabbat dinner every week with their devoted family, and sometimes additional guests. She attracts people because she is engaged in her days—natural and real, able to be aware of and manage the totality of her new life. She jokes about her "stumps" in one breath and muses about death in another. She is actively involved with her six grandchildren, and continues to be a loving, engaged wife, mother, grandmother, and friend.

There was a turning point for Lin a long time after her return home. We made much space for her grief and anger in our "God times," as we call them. She wanted to curse—or worse—at people who suggested that she focus on the positive, "since, after all," they told her, "You did not die." Lin is anything but a Pollyanna. We talked often about the need to trust and honor the darkness. It is only by going into God's shadow that we can find God's light. The womb of pain, rage, confusion, uncertainty can be holy. It may be the deepest truth in a person for a period of time. If we trust the timing of our hearts, it is likely that we will be organically lifted from mourning and rage. One day, perhaps eighteen months after Lin's health crisis, she said she wanted to talk about how she might possibly use her physical handicap for the good. She'd had a thought that felt God-given. She could put people at ease with the disabled if they seemed squirmy, she suggested. She would initiate contact by being friendly. She'd talk to strangers, smile at them, joke with them. She would name the elephant in the room, indirectly or directly if necessary. Lin's life led her into devastation. She has allowed her challenges to teach her, and she is teaching others.

Chapter 7: Waking Up Again and Again

Entering and Emerging

It is only through compassion that one can live with the contradictions within oneself and others, and...realize the harmonizing beauty of the human soul.
—Sanford Drob, Kabbalistic Visions: C. G. Jung and Jewish Mysticism

It's small, our winter home, our annual retreat.
Two bedrooms, two bathrooms. Too much

joy, we joke, as we sit on the balcony,

too much gratitude to contain. The carpet

is stained.

In about six spots. Small stains,
not like
in our marriage, where the stains

are large—from the times when we both—
thinking we were so wise—were so foolish.

Stains no amount of bleach or borax, reflection
or remorse, can erase. Perhaps

like Jacob, we entered into faithfulness,
then were spun around to probe the Other Side.

Entering *and* emerging—I learn, through studying

the Zohar—is the challenge. Those who return

from the Other Side are very loved. By the Holy One.
Never stop talking, or listening, is the sacred invitation.

Even now, as we sit on our balcony
above the ocean,

and regard one another and our old bodies
with tender humor,

light pours
in all day.

Suffering Is Not Always "Neurotic"—Besides, Neurotic Can Be Good

For most people, *neurosis* is a dirty word. Jung's view was that an outbreak of neurosis is purposeful, an opportunity to become conscious of who we are, as opposed to who we think we are. By working through the symptoms that invariably accompany neurosis—anxiety, fear, pain, guilt, and particularly conflict—we become aware of our limitations and discover our true strengths. Neurosis, Jung believed, is really an attempt at self-cure.

In my time of dread, I simply could not stop my looping thoughts. It seemed my suffering was caused by my mind, but, to this day, more than two years later, I do not know what caused my anguish. I believed then, and still do, that my suffering—a spiritual emergency of a sort—was trying to help me heal. Perhaps a call from the Divine to keep walking toward the ever-moving target of wholeness. My anguish may also have been my body/soul saying something like, "Sweetheart, there is something terribly wrong in your body. Prepare yourself." (In my mind, God often calls me "Sweetheart.") As painful as it was, I saw the four-month period of dread as a call to awaken, to understand and work with what was happening. To know, no kidding, that I am in control of very little. I prayed a lot. Felt anxious a lot. Cried a lot. And eventually, the breakthrough—of sorts. At the time, I felt I had no choice, that God had locked me into my inner chamber with my dread and said, "Get to know one another. Become friends," but looking back I see I *did* choose to stay present to the darkness. Showing up daily to hear what writing this book was telling me, was one way. And when I was diagnosed with colon cancer, two weeks after the darkness lifted, I no longer felt torn apart with the kind of opaque, confused anguish I had so recently experienced. I had God with me once more. I also felt blessedly a little clearer and stronger. I had stayed present to God's and my own darkness and in remarkable moments experienced God's light. I felt sad and soft and open much of the time, and my family told me I was simple and immediate. Openly expressed vulnerability can be a gift to everyone.

The damn thing, though, is that it is almost inevitable that I will be grinding my teeth in agony and confusion sometime in the future. Our complexes, our neuroses, our very human wobbles are never cured. Sometimes, I will not be "neurotic" but simply in the healthy and pure pain of Suffering One. Sometimes, I will fall again into Suffering Two, that crazy country where I am trapped in anguished, looping thoughts, or nasty self-recriminations. It becomes easier, though, to escape the claws of the demons, each time we tenderly befriend our squirrely parts and make a place for our wounds. The word *Israelite* means "God-wrestler."

It is occasionally true, too, that it is possible to drop-kick —far, far away—the nasty places in us. This may be another way of saying "tough love."

Go for It

Alan had back surgery in May 2003. We were hopeful that it would eradicate the stenosis in his spinal column and cure his sciatic pain. We were optimistic that he would walk freely after surgery. However, his pain did not abate, and indeed worsened over time. We consulted many experts and were told that recovery might continue for at least a year. But when Alan

Chapter 7: Waking Up Again and Again

and I saw the surgeon six months after the surgery, we all had to acknowledge that the operation had been a failure. In this visit, the surgeon suggested that he redo the operation, only deeper and wider. An alarming thought, but the phrase "Go for it" came instantly to my mind. I said nothing to Alan. A few days later, Alan told me that he was leaning toward having the surgery and asked what I thought. I told him I had received an instant "Go for it." I asked if he had been praying for guidance. "Yes," he said. He is not someone who usually prays.

Alan had the second surgery in 2004. He has had almost no sciatic pain since then, and indeed, in 2020, when I write this, although he still has severe stenosis, he has not had another back operation. At eighty he has body "issues," as we remark wryly, but he is fit and well and still plays knockout golf with frequently remarkable scores. We have declared the operation a success.

I reflected many times after that second surgery on the fact that I had had such a strong leaning toward "Go for it." Listening is a primary practice. If I get some words that seem distinctly "other," I pay attention.

Nothing Special

> **Man can be said to create God.**
> —Sanford Drob, *Symbols of the Kabbalah*

Rooted to the seat.
The third movement
of Rachmaninov's second
vibrates
my body and the car
like a tuning fork.

An old man with a walker
and a dusty black fedora
looks this way
and that
at the stoplight
on Lawrence.

Tips his hat to a young woman
and begins his trek
across the road.

It is nothing special
and yet...my mouth
goes all twisty, my eyes
fill with tears, and my sweetheart
smiles and says

*There she goes
again,*

Chapter 7: Waking Up Again and Again

*making something
out of Nothing*

Whisper within the Whisper: A Prayer-Poem

(There is) the startling experience of encountering the faces of the Divine, as they move from abstraction to living presence.
—Melila Hellner-Eshed, *Seekers of the Face*

Help me listen
for the whisper

within the whisper—

soft sound
of sea-wash

against a rock
of ages—
so old,
I cannot behold
it without bowing.

Help me know,
as I know *anything*,

that this terrible
tenderness
in my heart,
for the hurt
of humanity,

and the hope
for healing,

which never dies,

is You.

CHAPTER 8: TOUCHING UNITY: THE LIGHT OF GOD'S DARKNESS

A Double Helix

The flow of light out of supreme darkness
—Arthur Green, *Judaism for the World.*

We walk slowly
  down the hill,
dragging
our feet. It is hot, late
fall as we approach
our destination,
this cemetery
buried
in the hills of Jerusalem.
I am lost
in heartbreak and dread.

We thread our way
between gravesites, people
crowded in death
as they were in life
standing at the holy
Wall, swaying, fierce
in their sorrow, gratitude,
entreaties.

Now on Alan's left

The Light of God's Shadow

I perch
on a rickety bench. Ilana
sits feet away
on the concrete
beside her husband's—our
son's—grave.

How does a mother
lose a child? He was in my body,
now he is in the ground.

The sun beats
down.
Slow tears
glisten my cheeks.
We sit in silence.

After a long while I stand,
stumble between the gravesites
toward the boundary
of the cemetery.
Just beyond the wall
in a field sparse with grass, a tree
is shrouded in white fall flowers.
The branches look—for heaven's sake—like
the Goddess Kali or a ballerina
with several arms like wings
curved upward.
The royal cerulean sky
floats with wisps of clouds.

Seized at once
by the proclamation of life,
I bless the wild
beauty of the Kali tree,
the sky and clouds
ever in motion,
a solitary bird coasting
on an updraft of breath,

while nearby our boy
lies.

I am turned
inside out and taken
beyond all I know

as life and death
braid

in this very moment

into a blessed, cursed
double helix.

Velvet Blackness

Very soon after I had completed the first week of my training to become a gestalt therapist, when I was thirty-three, I began to experience intense, unusual anxiety. Somewhat familiar with my knee-jerk reaction of "uh-oh, danger" to anxiety or sorrow, and knowing that anxiety is often a soul signal of something calling for attention, I called my friend Ruth, an uncommonly wise therapist. She invited me to her house that night. Ruth kindly listened to all I could think of that might be causing anxiety—all my theories and conjectures—but offered none of her own. Rather, she invited me to shut my eyes and be quiet. Very reluctantly, I did. I felt immediately terrified and opened my eyes instantly. Gently, Ruth invited me into myself again. Blackness. Alarming blackness. Nothing else. I opened my eyes quickly. Ruth suggested once more that I go in and down—into my body and my heart—that I temporarily leave my thinking head. After several forays into and out of emptiness, I was able to stay—with pounding heart—present to myself. Absolute stillness. I felt as if I were floating down and down, into a darkness I had never known. After what felt like forever, I came to a place where I discovered to my shock and joy that the blackness was soft, velvety. I was okay. I was alone in there and not alone. I was held in love.

We need to be present to our hearts, to listen to our anguish, our confusion, our rage. Our yes and our no. Our emptiness and nothingness. There may be no more important way to love ourselves.

We also need to listen deeply to the Great Mother when she howls in pain and rage, for our beloved planet is in dire trouble. We need to grieve with the earth, the sea, with all forms of life. We need to recognize more of our responsibility for our brothers and sisters. We need to find our unique story in the story of the world. When, each time, we stay with the velvet darkness—and the timing and process will be different for everyone—we may find more psychospiritual maturity, the strong softness that calls for action. Then we need to do something concrete—the action of love in the world.

Be Still and Know

The greatest wish of the Zohar is to awaken...humanity...to a more expansive and divine perception of reality.
—Melila Hellner-Eshed, A River Flows from Eden

Be still and know that I am God. (Psalm 46:10)

Throw away
the martinis

and marbles
and cigarettes
and chewing gum.
Stop rocking
the chair.

Go in
      and down.

You may encounter bumpy
roads, dust,
even a scorpion.

But if you are still
long enough,
the stories
that have waited
your entire life,
will find you.

Welcome
your tears,
the howls
of rage,
the velvet silence—

And then,
like after
a rainstorm,
where dust
has been lovingly
patted down,
you may
smell something

that puts you in mind
of frangipani.

You may
hear the sun
yawning hello,

and may notice, with wonder,
that you, indeed,
are a thing of beauty.

Nature and Noticing

Matthew Fox is an Episcopal priest and founding president of the University of Creation Spirituality in California. He suggests that creativity is the key to our genius and beauty as a species. Also, to our capacity for evil. We need to manage this God-given gift with intention. Many undergo their most profound mystical experiences during acts of creativity. He suggests that entering the dark, being in intimate relationships, learning to praise, and deepening our gratitude are all acts of creation.

In his inspiring book *Original Blessing*, Fox teaches that humans are not born with "original sin," as many Christians were taught, but are born blessed. His invitation is to pay attention as we walk through our days, to celebrate existence. The Divine, he tells us, loves witness and acknowledgment. When we have an attitude of curiosity to life, we may conclude that the Holy One is winking at us, prodding us, and dropping hints and clues—in nature, in things people say, in television commercials. Discernment of invitations from the Divine can be a full-time job. "What now, my Love?" we can profitably chant, a thousand times a day.

Every day, if I can, I take a contemplative walk. In Florida, where we spend our winters, I pray with my feet on the edge of sea and sand. In this liminal space I simply attend to the day's shoreline. Marco Island's beaches are often studded with shells, and there are times when walking is a challenge for bare feet. It depends on the tides and the moon. But walking is one of my covenants, and paying attention to this ever-changing natural world is a commitment to presence. Convenience has no place in a life lived with faithfulness. How can we love only when life is gentle? Walking the same path every day is a fine spiritual practice. When we do, we can befriend and become intimate with our daily landscape and witness tiny changes. Besides, as we are taught, you can never step in the same ocean twice.

    For many years I prayed during the entire walk—prayers from Hebrew liturgy, petitionary and intercessory prayers. One day I realized that this was a way to avoid being alone. If I did not enter deep silence, how could I ever wonder whether it was the transcendent whispering to me or just my eager mind? In the nonstop talking to God, I could also sidestep the darker places for which silence might be an express elevator into the abyss. Many avoid being completely alone, for fear of the nothingness in them. I stopped the rote praying on my daily walk, and tried to stay empty, open, curious.

    Since my epiphany of running from God, each day is different. Sometimes I feel a tiny bit more awake. Sometimes I spend my walk in a place of darkness that seems unrelated to anything. I may feel stuck, messy, anxious. I reflect on dreams, on what to prepare for dinner, on what to add to the shopping list. Melodies arrive. I experience ecstatic flashes. I talk to the Source of Life: "Hey, Beloved. Get a load of this naked toddler. How did you know to make the human tush so beautiful? And check out those pelicans flying in formation, the leader so graceful, the three huge birds so perfectly in slipstream." I walk a long time, often without thought. Blessedly quiet, empty. This is worship—openness to all thoughts, feelings, perceptions, and musings. This is sacred witness as nature does its thing. This is the Divine as immanence and transcendence, present in every moment. The very act of daily walking and studying the Divine in the constant process of transformation affords me the gift of awakening.

The Blessing of Mike

I met Mike one day when walking the beach in Florida. I was doing exercises to improve my posture, lifting my arms to shoulder height, opening and stretching my shoulder blades—East and West—careful not to make my upper back concave. Grinning cheerfully, Mike called from the shallow waters, "Are you under arrest?" I liked him immediately. He was one of the "regulars"—a daily walker, like me. We regulars all have our own reasons for walking. Most of us are introverts. Mike's slow, steady walk, calf-deep in the ocean, was a kind of meditation, although he looked more like an aged prizefighter than a mystic. He was purportedly looking for shells for his grandkids. Over the years I knew him, I never once saw Mike pick up a shell. I liked the look of his suntanned and strangely scarred body. My guess was that he had been well-used by life, that he had taken and given a lot.

Although I cherish solitude, whenever I saw Mike, I would wade into the water to meet him halfway so we could chat about this and that for a few moments. He was open, natural, devoid of pretense. Early on in our conversations, he told me that he had made a mess of his early life. "Shit," he said, "I drank too much and wore my wife down. She gave up on me and I can't say I blame her." He went on to say that now he was doing his best to make amends to his kids, his grandkids, and even to his wife with whom he was still in contact. Whenever he received the call for a babysitting gig, Mike would fly from Marco Island to be Grandpa wherever he was needed, often for several weeks. He had kids and grandchildren around the country. "Shit, taking care of my grandchildren is the least I can do," he offered. I liked Mike a lot. His gritty authenticity was nourishing. He was doing *tikkun*, repair for the damage he had caused. If I would have said that to him, he would have probably said, "Shit, what are you talking about?" Instead, I told him I liked him because he was weird, like me. I meant spiritual.

Last year marked the third or fourth year that Mike and I had become beach buddies of a sort. One day he suggested that he and Alan and I go for dinner somewhere on the island. It was a great idea, but Alan and I were leaving the next day. "Next year, Mike, as long as one of the three of us hasn't croaked," I joked.

The following year I looked for Mike every day as I walked my worship. One morning I saw Lucy for the first time of the season. She is a regular walker who lives year-round on Marco Island. She's the beach mama—knows everyone, all the comings and goings of the snowbirds. We greeted each other warmly and joked about the fact that we had both made it through another year. I asked about Mike and wondered if he was doing another of his grandpa gigs. Lucy told me sadly that he had had a massive fatal heart attack that summer.

I had been looking forward to learning more about what made Mike so unabashedly committed to redemption. I wanted to joke with him about life and about being a grandparent. I wanted to boast about our nineteen grands and ten great-grands. It was too late. I was deeply, deeply saddened. I still am. May Mike's memory be a blessing. I want to say that I will learn from this experience, that I will not let such sweet opportunities slip away in the future. I wish I could be sure that this is true.

Squeaky Clean Is Not So Desirable

I have much gratitude for dreams, for I believe they tell us what we need to hear. In every session, I ask my directees

The Light of God's Shadow

if they have had a dream. Many begin remembering them. The dreams issue from the unconscious, the deep wisdom, the divine spark within, saying, "Listen up. Talk about this. There are important clues here to help you wake up."

I am working in spiritual direction with Nancy whose mother is dying. Nancy is someone who remembers her dreams, and almost always has one the night before our session. The dream that occurs the night before a spiritual direction session is especially important. Nancy's mother, Lacey, by all accounts, is a cross between Bea Arthur and Mother Teresa. A sassy, big-mouthed dame with a heart to match—all love in action. The kind of mother we all want. And Lacey is dying. Fairly imminently. In the session, Nancy, one of life's super-achievers, talks for a long time about her work as a social worker. I notice her looking often at the large clock I have in my room. Her body is tense, her left leg jiggles. Nancy's usual impeccable attire is less than perfect today—a tiny stain on her white blouse, hair not in the usual tidy ponytail. She is not wholly present. Toward the end of our time Nancy reports the following dream: *I see a huge teacup. It is so big I can just see over the top. I notice a tiny creature on the rim of the cup. I look inside the cup and notice some grains and a little debris on the bottom of the cup. I have an impulse to clean up this small mess, but my intuition tells me not to. I ignore the quiet voice and reach inside the cup. In so doing, I knock the little creature to the bottom. I am surprisingly heartbroken. I reach inside the cup, lift up the tiny creature, and place it on my upturned palm. The creature stirs. I feel great relief, even joy.*

No person can know how another should be, but the Dream Maker often has very strong ideas. We ignore these at our peril. Nancy's unusual dream was strangely compelling. One of those big dreams. If we try to keep life squeaky clean, never to have messes in our lives or in our hearts, we risk killing our spirit. If we try to clean up perfectly the debris at the bottom of the cup, we will likely keep making the same mistakes in life. Uncertainty, unknowing, and messiness are part of our lives.

I wonder aloud with Nancy if there is something she isn't talking about, whether her frequent looking at the clock bespeaks some anxiety. Nancy is silent for several moments. "It's my mom," she finally says. "Her death is closer. A miracle is not likely. I am angry that she has cancer. She refuses pain medication because she wants to be alert 'til the end. There is no point in my praying. No point crying," she says. We sit quietly.

After a while I ask if I may pray. "Yes," Nancy says.

I am silent and listen into myself to what wants to be said. A prayer of intention like this, born in the moment, is created in the sacred space between the Divine, the person, and me. I never know what we will hear. This is how my poems arrive. "Dear God, I pray for Lacey to be as comfortable and alert as possible. I pray that being with her beloved family brings her deep solace. She is a woman of faith. I pray she can feel Your presence. May she feel blessed. Now, Holy One, I turn my prayer to Nancy. Please may she feel her soft strength in this time of such loss and sorrow. Please may the great love between Nancy and her mother be vibrantly alive as Lacey moves through these difficult days, and may it continue to live in Nancy forever. And please, Beloved, if it is possible, may Nancy feel Your presence here, now. Amen." We are silent. Nancy's leg stops moving and after a short while she surrenders to long, shuddering sobs, her nose running freely. I cry, too. Such love. When our time is up, we hug, and Nancy leaves. Nancy's tears are a prayer, a surrender to grief. The dream invited her to be less tidy in the service of her soul. She honored this.

At times, we sleepwalk through life. It may be hard to stay awake to the bigness of the moment, except very briefly. Perhaps there is no brighter light but that which emerges from darkness. The more we awaken, the more we see how the whole world can shine, even in times of heartbreak. When we are openhearted with the reality of life's darkness and our own dear imperfect psyches, we may be more able to feel the love that underlies all existence. Nancy's is an example of a dream from the collective unconscious that has meaning for us all.

Chapter 8: Touching Unity: The Light of God's Darkness

Courtesan

A person who has the ability to receive our words with an open mind and no agenda of their own, (offers holy witness.)
—Tirzah Firestone, Wounds into Wisdom

Not the prettiest, nor most
shapely.
But the most sought-after.

She sewed all her own clothes.
Soft colors. Blue. Lilac. Ecru.
Wore her hair, gray at the temples,
short, tidy, close to her head.

When she disrobed, she turned,
head slightly tilted,
as if listening for something.
Asked soft questions—
about their children, jobs,
even their wives.

The light in the room was just
right—neither too bright,
nor too dim.
The music—Brahms, Chopin.
Puccini.
Some men sighed as soon as she touched
them. Occasionally even cried.

The other girls did not know why,

The Light of God's Shadow

but they, too, felt easy with her.
Some even confided in her.
When she spoke,
she said neither too little,
nor too much.

Asked once why
she was a courtesan,
she thought a while,
then quietly said, "I don't
know. It just feels right."

And the men—one surprised himself
by confiding in his sister, one solemn
and lonely day. "I don't know,"
he said, "but it feels like
being loved by God."

Temporal Language

I am speaking of this One that was there "before" the Big Bang, if one may use temporal language at all.
—Arthur Green, Essay: *Judaism as a Path of Love*

One shouldn't.

Try, that is,
to wrap one's words
around infinity.

Or love.
Or God.

Yet one cannot cease.

Because unless one
can form sounds and vowels
that are breathed
into the night sky
like nightingales
echoing into
mountains

or find perfect
words to write
about
the pinprick
of light
of a lone star

The Light of God's Shadow

in a gentle night—

one may only
wring
helplessly
one's hands.

Chapter 8: Touching Unity: The Light of God's Darkness

God's Hammock

On one of our annual trips to the holy land, Alan and I are buying clothes for our four Canadian granddaughters. Tali is our saleswoman, all Israeli charm—young, outspoken, cheerful, and brassy. She persuades us to take two dresses, headbands, and berets for each girl. Eight dresses in all. The same dress for Maya and Hannah, because Hannah wants to be just like her big cousin Maya when she grows up. Tali is sassy and funny, superb at her job. At some point I notice a Hebrew tattoo on her arm. I ask her to translate. "Only God can judge me," she says.

I often think of Nancy's mystical dream about the teacup and her soul, the dream that guided her to embrace life's messiness. It was a wise message. I wish her dream could transform me. But no dream—nothing—teaches me once and for all to hold life's difficulties with consistent ease. Life and I are both messy. When awake, I'm with Tali—God is my only judge. I do my best to be human, uncluttered, kind. When asleep, I am sometimes prosecutor, jury, and judge, full of unkind comments about my imperfections. Waking up is a lifetime's opus. My ability to hold life's vagaries and vicissitudes with at least a modicum of equanimity and the absence of negative self-commentary is a work in progress. Resting in God's hammock is more likely to occur when we catch the mean, snarky, self-critical one speaking from his hiding place and boot him out. I always think of the nasty one in my psyche as being male since I met Chip Henderson in a dream. God, the deepest wisdom in our Self should be the only judge. Jazzy Tali knew that, and her very presence radiated light.

The World-to-Come

Forgetting is the norm.
—Michael Fishbane, Sacred Attunement

I yawn, stretch, squint
at the old clock
on the dresser.
Red numbers glow

in the velvet black—
6:03 on this day,
Tuesday, November 20,
of this year, 2018.

Here, now, the river
flows from Eden,
my breath flows
from me,

and in this next minute
of big, red numbers—6:04—
I am breathed
once more.

Creation is doing its thing, and
in this seventy-five-year-old
moment, I am
alive—
continuous

Chapter 8: Touching Unity: The Light of God's Darkness

with

the clock,
the sounds of the morning
yawning,
the brisk air against
my face,
the rumpled
bedcovers.

I rise,
gather my old
terry-cloth robe

around me, think
about heaven
and
making coffee.

There will never

again be 6:07—
as it is now,
and now, 6:08

in red numbers
that glow
in the velvet black—

on this day, Tuesday,

The Light of God's Shadow

November 20,
2018. I pray I may
remember
the miracle—

the world-to-come
is being created,
now and now
and now.

Chapter 8: Touching Unity: The Light of God's Darkness

Love and Gratitude

My friend Laura and I are having one of our spiritual friendship visits on Zoom—Laura in California, me in Toronto. As soon as I see her, I become tearful—gratefully. These days there is a constant underground river of sorrow in me about Eli's death. I know that all my emotions will be welcome in our sacred space, because of the deep and intimate connection Laura and I have, and because of Laura's psychospiritual maturity. I tell her that I keep asking, "How could this happen?" I am silent for a few minutes. Laura, too. "I *know* how it happened," I go on to say. "Eli had advanced liver disease. But *how* could it happen?" Laura is deeply present, quiet, and tender with my rawness. I cry and we talk about Eli for a long time.

Laura knows I am a good crier, that I have learned—over all the years of traveling with my wholeness and brokenness—to allow the pain to move in and through me. I trust grief. Each brief or lengthy cycle of mourning leaves me both wrung-out and new—open to the beauty of Eli's soul and the privilege of being his mother. Also open to the wonder of life itself. I tell Laura again that he was an extraordinary person, of uncommon gifts and beauty. I would not have known quite how beautiful but for his death, I say. I speak of Eli's family, of how their capacity to celebrate life may have become even more spirited. I tell her of Moishe, Eli and Ilana's youngest son. Of how his bar mitzvah was honored, despite Eli's death seven months earlier. We talk of how tragedy and exquisite beauty sometimes occur simultaneously, of how acceptance of life's paradox and complexity enriches our souls. The light of God's shadow. For both of us, and for many, there may be no way to get closer to mystery but through the landscape of great pain and great surrender. If you *feel* the sorrow, we agree, your world may open to something so enormous and beautiful, it gentles and blesses your grief.

When I am done talking and crying, my heart softens and spreads wider. From Jewish mysticism I learn that searing openness between two or more may bring us closer to the very breath of existence. I tell Laura that her dear face is shining and she tells me mine is, too. I am filled with love—it starts with her and spreads out in concentric circles, like ripples in a pond. I think of our beloved Israeli and Canadian families, of people dancing in the rain, of others struggling to pay their bills. It often happens like this. I grieve deeply and openly, and when I am done for this round, all I feel is love and gratitude. Laura tells me of the image she has received. Laura is the queen of images. "Have you ever been to the Grand Canyon?" she asks. I nod. She sees the two of us standing at the edge looking into the bottomless void. We are holding hands, silently contemplating the indescribable grandeur. "It's as if the Grand Canyon is the Divine and life, and we are on the edge of something both overwhelmingly exquisite and terrifying. That is how God is," she smiles crookedly. "You don't know or understand anything, and yet you have to have all your experiences and feelings, anyhow." We sigh sweetly in unison.

In Quiet Love

The world gives itself in quiet love, to the spirit of the human...
—Michael Fishbane, Jewish Hermeneutical Theology

You lie for a while
    on a sunny
        then cloudy
   then sunny day,

a blade of sweet
grass
between
your teeth.

Existence
comes into being
then dissolves

as clouds
    pulsate
        shimmer
   morph
  from shape
      to shape.

These moments in time
   join hands
with
eternity
as your eyes

The Light of God's Shadow

almost closed,
study
    the sky.

      A dinosaur,
an eggcup,
a rose-
bush.

Uncle Harry's hat.
Your favorite
aunt Sadie's
face
    before
she died

and—just in time—
  her granddaughter
Sarah
was born.

Chapter 8: Touching Unity: The Light of God's Darkness

Small Bites and Chew Nicely

I am lying on the table at Sunnybrook Hospital. Jamie and Andrew, the radiation therapists, have ensured that the radiation machine is aligned with my colon tumor, that my legs are straight, my arms tucked next to my body. They measure something on my body and call out complex numbers to each other. It is very otherworldly. Then Andrew nods and says, "Here we go," and they leave the room, shutting the heavy door that protects them from radiation. I close my eyes and prepare for the burning to take place. One of our doctor friends told us that the treatment for cancer is sometimes referred to as "slash, poison, and burn"—surgery, chemotherapy, and radiation. I laughed when I heard this. I pray for the success of the treatment and become quiet. I am peaceful, as if the radiation therapy is the hand of God. I cried during the first time I was burned, but not since. The phrase "Here we go" feels like the Beloved telling me that something awful but necessary is happening. Indeed, I feel a warmth in my heart. Although alone, I am not alone. I sometimes even feel the light of God's darkness, a unity of many hopes and feelings, as my dear belly is being burned by poison. When I feel the unity, I am deeply peaceful.

I do not believe that the Holy One gave me cancer. Nor do I believe that God will take it away. In truth, as I continue to befriend my raw vulnerability, I know more than ever that I don't know what God is. I just know that I love the Holy Blessed One with all of me. Every breath I take is a gift. My humility feels grace given. All I need to live is this small moment, one radiation treatment, one day of chemotherapy medication at a time. All I need to do is try to be as awake to the moment as I can. All I need to do is try to discern the desire of the Holy One for me, so I can learn what I can learn. "My Love," I pray often, "what now? What do you want of me in this very moment?" All I have is my experience in these luminous days before surgery—a warmth and a rush of sensation in my belly and heart as I walk through my days greeting people, praying for other cancer patients, counting my good fortune to be at this hospital with such a superb reputation. Feels suspiciously like love.

Although he prided himself on his left-leaning, modern attitudes, my father was a God-fearing man in a surprisingly primitive way. So vulnerable to shame, he almost never visited a synagogue because of his inability to read Hebrew. His image and that of his family were so important to him. A man of many shalts and shalt-nots, Dad drilled us in table manners and courtesy at the nightly dinner table. "Elbows off the table. Small bites and chew nicely." Kind and considerate, my father was a compassionate listener, and he had a sweet sense of humor. He awakened his three daughters each morning with a playful, intentionally foolish poem. Much of what I received from my father was a huge blessing. The anxiety and fear of anxiety were not.

Do I trust that I will ever become the ouroboros, the snake or dragon that swallows its own tail, a symbol of wholeness and healing? I have learned through my prolonged period of suffering that—as one of my big dreams told me—there will likely be many more seeds of uncertainty and unknowing to plant in my life. There will be other times I will find myself in the room of my dream and will have to work harder than usual at waking up. My time of dread, the cancer treatment, COVID-19, and Eli's death have taught me to live a little differently with darkness and anxiety, uncertainty and unknowing. I have experienced blessed moments and occasionally even more than just moments of feeling whole, connected to the Source of Life.

But it's an ongoing story, so, to mix metaphors shamelessly, if I keep planting the seeds and take small bites and chew nicely, I might just manage.

The Word *Lyrical*

Creation is latent with layers of mystery, a world of secrets.
Nothing is the way it appears.
—Lawrence Kushner. *Kabbalah: A Love Story*

The word
shows up—a waking
dream—in swaths
of sultry breathing
around and through me, blessing
this moment in time.

I believe I am supposed
to do something with the word
but in truth
this is an ordinary moment. My lower
back throbs unbecomingly, and the grandfather
toe on my right foot itches mysteriously.
The humidity of this early Tuesday morning
is steamy and sulky
yet I keep thinking
lyrical.

I search for pictures
in my mind
to tell you
of Eden, lush with waterfalls
both thundering and gentle, source
of the famous river that flows
into each moment of existence.

But all I see is sullen clouds
and petulant sweet peas.
I try to imagine Stravinsky pacing—left
foot, right foot—as music appears
on lined paper in green
ink—as a dream revealed
last night. But I hear only August
cicadas, protesting the heat,
and the barely audible hum
of the universe always saluting
silence.

I pray
for words to shine
with such delicacy that your
eyes will shut and you will imagine
one flutter of a Monarch against
a blazing giant sunflower,
or the tip of a stamen
waltzing dizzily
on an orange daylily.
Perhaps you will remember
the catch
in your throat
when you looked at your adult
son, glasses perched
on his nose,

and you will think.
lyrical.

The Light of God's Shadow

But my words come from
my bowels with their own baggage,
and all you will likely imagine
is a ponderous turtle—
left foot, right foot—
and the sounds
of jackhammers and whining
saws.

It's like this at times,
when broken open
with wonder
I pull you close
to me, pressed
against my right side, so we may gaze
in awe
at life before us
in this very moment.
Sigh sweetly in unison.
But all I can think
as we stand—in breath
out breath—is how hot it is,
and how soon I can sidle
into solitude.

Chapter 8: Touching Unity: The Light of God's Darkness

Leaving the Room—for Now

My friend Kristen and I are having one of our Zoom conversations. She's in Singapore, I'm in Toronto. We met when we were both on the Coordinating Council of Spiritual Directors International. Deeply committed to *shmutz* cleaning as a primary wake-up practice, to facing life and ourselves honestly, Kristen and I have learned together to grow in deep honesty, to say tough things, and to hear each other without defending or explaining ourselves. A gift.

I talk with Kristen about the last two years, so intense and frequently painful. I tell her how I often felt that I was in the room of my dream, where I was called to be intensely awake. "I thought my book would be poems celebrating and honoring my beloved six," I say. "Instead, I was thrust into two years of deep interiority because of life's happenings. I was asked to surrender to what the Holy One and the book wanted of me. Yes, I was to write my love poems to my six. And urgently, I was also called to reflect on my life, to develop a different relationship with my own shadow, and God's.

"It was the worst two years of my life," I continue. "I had no choice but to stay in my room, my inner sanctum, in deepest connection with my soul. During this time of large and small traumas, I connected with my six from time to time, by email, phone calls, and occasional Zoom conversations. Like you, they were immensely kind about my tales of DRECC, which was my four-month stint of being shackled to *dread*, the shock and pain in the world when the blinders of systemic *racism* and brutal societal inequality were ripped off. *Eli's* three-month illness and then death. My *colon cancer*, the treatment, and ongoing recovery. And, finally, COVID-19. I also shared some of my joys and gratitude with my six, my celebrations and even some of my dreams."

I'm on a roll now, and Kristen's warm attention blesses me. "As you know, I often experience the Divine in both frightening and wondrous ways, and my primary desire is to keep waking up. Indeed, seen through a different lens, the room of my dream was a sanctuary for my injured soul, a place of healing and ingathering." Kristen asks me to talk about just one thing I have learned. "I'll tell you two," I answer. "Life does its thing. Good stuff and bad stuff. While we have tons of responsibility for living well and mindfully, most often we have no control over what happens to us. I am always learning that I am riding shotgun, not driving the bus. I know this now more than ever. I can therefore relax a *little* more easily into whatever life tosses my way. And I still feel like an earnest student. I am beginning to roll the word "equanimity" around in my mouth.

"I have also learned that there is always *something* I can do. I can attempt to feel God in my breath. I can roll up my sleeves and intensify my attempts to learn from what is occurring. I can pray 'What now, my Love?' a million times a day. During my four-month time of dread, I was in the desert, and I could not see God's face or hear God's voice. My dreams were sparse. That was the worst. But after the strange time of dread passed, even though there were new and horrible nasties to deal with, even though Eli's death was beyond heartbreaking, even though my cancer was not a picnic, I felt connected to the Divine. My prayers usually brought a sense of connection."

'What now, my Love?' may be my baseline question to the Holy One in good and bad times. 'What do You want of me now? What am I to learn in this moment?' The prayer turns me toward God and helps me look for meaning in my suffering. I have learned so much—again," I tell Kristen. "I have learned that when I am in trouble, I can do my best to wake up more. And when I keep working my stuff, sometimes I become filled with light, love, wonder, gratitude—the light of God's shadow. But life, like air, is not static, so I do not stay in ecstasy. Light fades. And once more, the call is to wake up."

Unity: The Light of God's Darkness

I had a strangely beautiful snippet of a dream that felt like another oracle or telegram from the deepest place. It simply said: *The Light of God's Darkness*. I read a beautiful teaching from the Zohar to Alan. "Listen to this language," I say. "It makes me weep. I am not sure why, though I think it gets at the oneness of it all, how everything and its opposite exist in the Holy One."

When the Holy One created the world and wanted to reveal the depth within the hiddenness and the light from within the darkness, they were contained one within the other.

Alan frowns and says, "I don't understand a word." He beams at me and turns to sewing his latest backpack, the machine making a cheerful whirring sound.

If we live reflectively, we learn, from scripture and from our lives, of the shadow of the Divine and the violent, brutal, cruelty of life and of humans, as much as the overwhelming radiance, love and beauty of all. We realize that the light of God's darkness is not the light at the end of the tunnel. When we meet the shadow of the Holy One our work is not to look for the light. If we are able to live with the complexity and contradictions in life and welcome paradox, and polarity, we bless the light of God's darkness. Perhaps it is counterintuitive, but we may get to joy by staying with pain. Not relief but joy. The light of the dark. The experience of one enriches the other. The dream talks to the heartbreaking, heart-opening unity of the Holy One.

Blessedly, my life mostly showers me with light. Later this day, after sharing the Zohar snippet with Alan, I walk in my neighborhood. Each dear soul I encounter seems radiant—the gardener raking leaves who looks up and smiles shyly as I pass. The old woman who stops walking abruptly and searches anxiously through her oversized purse for her ringing phone. The family of three with four bumptious dogs. When I study God in my walk, I am almost always replenished. There is always something to be radically amazed about, as Rabbi Abraham Joshua Heschel taught.

There may be moments when, stalking our finitude, we become simultaneously aware of the gift and the fragility of loving. It is hard not to flee at these times, for the searing meeting with another when we love from the edge of our skin can almost hurt. Open, vulnerable, in the field of love, we know that love and loss are inextricably entwined. In these moments we may experience the sacred. There is no safety once you hold hands with your God-given love teachers. If we love unequivocally, our hearts will be broken open—more than once. The elemental and the concrete, the hidden and the revealed conjoin in rare moments. An everyday experience, like watching a child concentrate on creating a LEGO castle, becomes suspended in time, yet as immediate as a line in the palm of your hand—everything shimmering and humming. How do we bear such love?

One goal of an intentional life is to be mindful, intensely present in the now. As the cliché teaches, the older you are, the more quickly time disappears. I am sitting at the kitchen table savoring my morning coffee. I look at the family tree in pictures on the wall facing me. Alan's and my parents are at the top. Then Alan and me. Beneath us, our three sons, their wives, and their children. Our nineteen grandchildren and twelve great grands take up quite a lot of space. Alan updates the photos each year. To the right of Alan and me are the pictures of our siblings, and their children. There is also a photo of Stan, our friend who died so recently, and Ruthie, his wife and my "sister-by-choice," as I call her.

I study the wall and think of our beloveds who have died: Eli. Joan and Lionel, Alan's sister and her husband who both died very young. Our parents, of course. Stan. And suddenly I am filled with a love so blinding, for those who have gone and for the rest of us—each soul so unbearably beautiful—I feel "done in." It's one of those moments. I am intensely awake. I know that this is God. To live like this, to love like this, fills me with terror and humble wonder. I think, "It is all one. It is unity."

EMERGING: AN EPILOGUE

Progress Report

"Well," I report to my spiritual director Maureen, "for two years it felt as if I was in the room of my dream, in an unusually intense state of awakening. I often felt as if working with the book, trying to hear what the Beloved was teaching me, was saving my life. In some way I do not understand, my fidelity and dedication to the process of writing has been profoundly transformative. I definitely feel more awake now. The anxiety that seemed so daunting, so other, has shrunk considerably. I am even tasting ecstasy again from time to time. I know more than ever that I am not driving the bus. I even welcome uncertainty occasionally. And maybe most of all, I know that I am not cured of anything." My spiritual director listens intently. She knows the ways in which I have suffered for two years—the strange time of dread that lasted four months, my cancer, Eli's death. She also knows my proclivity to think I have found the secret of life. We talk about how all of this occurred in the time when COVID-19 had us all by the throat. We speak of how traumatic it has been for countless among us to live through these days. In this first visit together, post-COVID, we are even unmasked. No hug yet, though. I enthusiastically name what I have learned.

- To be human means we will suffer.
- Life can be pretty nasty at times. And ridiculously beautiful.
- If we work our *shmutz*, we may manage the nasties better when they occur. Not always, though.

- Working with dreams helps. As does having regular spiritual practices and creative work.
- Life goes better if we cooperate and give up the illusion of having control. This is maybe my main learning. My spiritual director, not being Jewish, rather likes when I say that the Rabbis teach us we have all of the responsibility, and none of the control.
- Reality requires us to plant seeds of uncertainty and unknowing many times in our lives. I am now on a first-name basis with Not-knowing.
- I understand, more than ever, the difference between neurotic suffering and real suffering. I mostly have compassion for my neuroses. Sometimes, though, I go into a complex about being in a complex.
- Jung said neurosis was an attempt at self-cure. Whenever I fall into one of my prolonged complexes or "attacks of neurosis," I hear this as a God-call. I have learned to call these times Crazy Country—I have never met anybody who does not have their own version of Crazy Country.
- Transformation occurs when we work with both our psychology and our relationship with the Divine, or whatever we name the greater-than-ourselves wisdom.
- A spiritual journey requires us to go deepest inside and get to know ourselves as we are. Then we are to go even deeper to where transcendent Self or God is providing ongoing instructions for waking up.
- Wake-up invitations come from the outside, too.
- I have faith in faith. Not in life turning out the way I want, for stuff happens. But faith that if I do daily

waking-up work, how I live will justify God's trust in me.
- The purpose of awakening is not happiness ever after or no anxiety at all.
- The purpose of being awake is to live in reality with consciousness and compassion.
- The final word is love.

"I think," I tell my spiritual director as an afterthought as I gather my belongings, "I have taken a noticeably big bite out of the elephant and may have even digested a bit of it. It has been a very painful and productive two years."

This is all very fine. I leave the session feeling quite satisfied and maybe even a wee bit pleased with myself. I do believe Maureen even nods approvingly.

This is Friday.

I wake up very early on Saturday morning. Just after 3:30. "Uh-oh," I think as I lie awake in a world-class state of anxiety.

"Hey, God," I mutter, "I thought I was done with all this nonsense."

Rowing Alone to an Island

We intentionally open ourselves to the pain in and around us without fleeing or defending ourselves.
—Tirzah Firestone, The Scapegoat

The boat is moored
nearby.
You know the task.

It is dark. The dark
you want
to pull around yourself
like a velvet wrap, though
it whispers
of aloneness.

There is just you
and a vastness that sings
in a language strange
and new.

In the emptiness you
know

you understand nothing,
and one day

there will be
no
you.

Emerging: An Epilogue

It is only then as you lie
on your back
with opened eyes and newly tender
heart
that you can see
the stars
held
in a sky
black with imploded
light, can breathe—deep
into the emptiness.

You rise,
get into the boat,
begin.

GIFTS FROM MY SIX

This whole book is a love letter to the Holy and to my six. You will have noticed that I also grumble to the Beloved a fair amount, too. With every poem you read, you spend time with my six. In the poems that I crafted from the magic of their prose you will learn how their teachings enter my heart. The gift to the world of their work is extraordinary. I am privileged to have connected personally with them, to be touched by their souls. It is my pleasure to offer just a little background about these fine people.

Sanford Drob, Tirzah Firestone, Michael Fishbane, Arthur Green, Melila Hellner-Eshed, and Lawrence Kushner have had an indelible impact on my journey of waking up. Their writings served as a source of inspiration as well as consolation during this remarkable period of my life, where I tasted more frequently both my brokenness and my wholeness. I am grateful for their wisdom as well as for their immense generosity in carving out time for conversations, email exchanges, and Zoom visits as I worked on this book.

When I think of my six, I often imagine being held within a circle, a unity of their energy and kindness. As you read, I hope that you, too, will feel held and supported by their wisdom and commitment to humanity. The poems below, attributed to each of them, are simply lifted from their beautiful prose.

Sanford Drob — Faith

In faith, one believes that *it just is*—
a kind of rock bottom that stands with us,
as does the very foundation
of the world.

Faith is the openness to what is most basic
and authentic about human experience—
a state of pure receptiveness, in which one

can tolerate fragmentation, meaninglessness,
blankness—the conditions for creativity and genuine
psychological birth, growth, and change.

One of Sanford Drob's passions, and mine, is the intersection of Jungian psychology and Jewish mysticism. In his book *Kabbalistic Visions. C. G. Jung and Jewish Mysticism*, Sandy writes "...the journey into the garden, as both Jung and Kabbalah well understood, must inevitably take us through the shadow world of the "Other Side." (p x) Sandy's writings about the shadow side of psyche and the Divine served me well during the time I felt captive to my darkness.

Although life can be humdrum, he mused in a conversation, in every moment there is the potential to lift up the blessed qualities of compassion, loving-kindness, grace, beauty, and morality. Or to bury them. Sandy knows when he is in a spiritual flow because his ethical, compassionate stance to the world is unusually alive and intense.

Sandy also accepts a layer of anguish as endemic to the human condition. He is acutely aware of the dark side of God and of the world. I told him about my "God-tears," one of my visceral invitations to pay close attention to the moment vibrating with the sacred. He said he gets God-tears when he listens to his prisoners. He has worked on a prison ward for over twenty years.

Sandy, like Lawrence Kushner, feels compelled to give expression to his soul through his painting. His art is his attempt to make the darkness of the world—past and present—as beautiful as possible. One of his repeated themes is the Holocaust. Sandy marries darkness and light in his paintings and in his work with the prisoners. He is working to create beauty out of the darkness and chaos of reality.

We spoke of how, in the psyche and in God, the opposites of light and dark shadow are foundational. When we are in conflict with these aspects within ourselves—say, between inherent kindness and a need to tougher—dreams and spiritual work can help us access the transcendent function, which may have aspects of both kindness and firmness but be bigger than either one. Sandy mused about how the unconscious mind knows things before the conscious mind does. He and I talked about our dreams, about how we collaborate with them. We all have a spark of the divine, he reminded me, and need to tune our radio to that frequency.

Sandy's writings remind me: Honoring the contrast between dark and light—and holding them both—is essential if we wish to live a life of wholeness. "A return to chaos and disorder," he teaches, "is a prerequisite for spiritual and psychological renewal" (*Kabbalistic Visions*, p. 52). If we are attuned to our souls and reality, we are compelled to do good because of the darkness.

Tirzah Firestone – The Snake

See the snake not as evil
but as the principle
of knowledge or emerging
consciousness.

The snake comes not to get us
into trouble, but to goad us
to know more, to uncover
our eyes

and through knowing become
more than we have been.
The snake is the part
that seeks self-
realization, to outgrow old points,
to shed our skin, and strive
for the wholeness that simply
will not brook

a one-sided
approach.

If we wish to lead a spiritual life, we need to wake up and to listen down low, Tirzah Firestone underscores—so we can find the wisdom beneath our feet. Our souls are always striving for wholeness, in every aspect of our lives. I discussed many of my dreams with Tirzah, and she was wise, inspiring and helpful. We muse together: What does Psyche or *Shekhinah* have to say? *Shekhinah*, the indwelling feminine of the Holy One, is evident in soup kitchens, random acts of kindness, and our own devotion to *shmutz* cleaning. The Divine Feminine is of the earth, the grit that houses the seedling as much as the food it brings forth— the manure and the heritage tomato.

Tirzah's passion for the feminine in mysticism led her to research women in the mystical tradition. The feminine approach to spirituality incorporates the inner spiritual life, and an attitude of openness and receptivity. "Women know in their cells and organs the work of...inward carrying...of stretching to the point of disfiguring themselves. ..to nurture a creation and bring it to life" (*The Receiving*, p. 99), she writes. The Divine needs us to bring heart and hands to the planet, for the Holy One does not have hands. Only we do.

Sometimes, she teaches, we learn to surrender to the Divine, and sometimes, like Abraham arguing with God at Sodom, we must wrestle. I spoke of my time of dread often with Tirzah, that wild, dark period in my life when I was blown asunder. I also shared with her my experience of love and awe-inspiring light. She was profoundly interested in my *walk into a room* dream where I tremble on the edge of unity, immersed in wonder and terror. Wonder and love often belong together, we agreed, as do terror and dread. I saw God's shadow, she suggested, and I felt terror.

Tirzah and I reflected often on the necessity to confront

and counter the dark side of God. We mused about my dream where I met Savage, the dark, uncivilized, chaotic aspect of life and of my psyche. We spoke of how God becomes God and evolves through humanity; of how the Divine needs us to incorporate darkness—both the Holy One's and our own. When we encounter the Self, the Godhead within the psyche, our bodies are overwhelmed, she told me. It is like plugging a turbojet into the socket fit for a washing machine. The circuitry is blown. Tirzah and I talk often with wonder and awe about both the radiance and darkness in our world. We also share a humility about always being beginners in our connection to God.

Michael Fishbane — A Chorus of Existence

In the holy Unfolding
there is song and speech.
It is sung by the heavens
and spoken by the earth,
day after day,
in ceaseless expressions
of light and sound
and birth and decay.
Each saying informs
every other:
the dying plants fertilize
the ground, the breath
of children revive
the earth, and there
is love and sorrow and
brute violence.

Michael Fishbane and I have talked about how every moment of life is sacred, how a primary commandment is to awaken to the presence, the call of the Holy One in ordinary life. It is so important, he believes, to take a spiritual stance toward "the mystery of the here and now of existence and its daily existential challenges" (*Fragile Finitude*, p. 47). He says "if you do not know the way yourself...seek other deposits of wisdom... Go to the place where truth is cultivated and learn wisdom from its teachers." (*Fragile Finitude*, p. 103).

Michael speaks often about how we are called by the Divine to be as kind as we can be, how we can develop empathy and humanity toward our fellow travelers—akin to Job's. Our awareness of our fragility and mortality may deepen our care for others. In one of our conversations, I went on a bit about my mantra of consciousness, choice, and kindness. Michael offered his perspective on the divine commandment: *limits and love*.

"Theology," he teaches, "is a spiritual practice, whose principal task is to guide human thought and sensibility toward God...to direct the human spirit toward . . . God as the heart and breath of all existence" (*Sacred Attunement*, p. 35). Theology is also a way of living, an attunement to the dailyness of life, a call to kindness. Michael is intent on living mindfully—life and time are sacred, he said.

Conversations with him, when I was in anguish after Eli died, brought me enormous comfort. I always felt closer to God and softer after talking with him. His kindness and spiritual wisdom and depth were immensely helpful, as were his offerings from his deep immersion in the richness of Jewish theology. Our connection brought me immense solace.

"When spiritual centeredness is real, pain finds its place," Michael told me. His writing is a profound spiritual activity for him, a way he "listens" and speaks. "Alertness is all," he teaches, "though forgetting is the norm." But if we are awake, our entire life becomes a form of prayer. Thoughts and speech and spiritual action should become as one gracious movement.

Michael has a concrete mystical orientation of trying to be present to the Divine in all ways, including ordinary life. I asked if he experiences the Divine. He said, "There are moments. Like when you see through the letters." It is about always looking through things to their deeper spiritual core. When these moments happen, it is a kind of verification that the path is unfolding. With an intensification of awareness, we become conscious of the miracle of presence. He writes, "God's worldly gifts open our mouths in response" (*Fragile Finitude*, p. 29). The Divine is always present, always in the process of becoming. The challenge is to pause, to approach life with a focused mind, so we may respond with an attitude of Attunement, a spiritual disposition. I am profoundly grateful to Michael for his enormous enthusiasm for my book which occurred when it was barely a seed and continued throughout all the years of the writing. The sensitivity of his soul and his gentle warmth were a blessing to me.

Arthur Green – There Is Naught But You

Our prayer is a cry
and a song to life itself,
called forth
from our innermost Self,
addressed to the wonder
and mystery of life,
that we have dared to call again
by the ancient and holy name
of God.

"To stand in God's presence is to live a life shaped by love," Arthur Green tells us (*Judaism for the World*, p. 92). "It requires an open heart, one that is able to receive the love of God that pours into each moment...to take in that blessing...and reshape it into love for those around us." Art speaks of humans, all living creatures, and the earth as potential recipients of our love. He teaches in a multitude of ways that the journey to the One is through the heart. His reverence is humble and awe-inspiring.

To connect with the Divine, to wake up, we go into our bodies, our *kishkes* (guts), our hearts and souls. Art believes that sometimes evil can be the result of our flight from our vulnerability which may create an awesome and frequently terrifying process. God is also struggling with God's own evil, and we, part of the great cosmic battle, must do so as well. "We... discover the Oneness of Being by staying right here, paying as close attention as we can to the present in which we live... The mystic offers us a journey inward, an inner opening rather than a vertical ascent" (*Ehyeh: A Kabbalah for Tomorrow*, p. 20).

I learn from Art, in rich, beautiful prose, how the Divine fills all of existence in the dailyness of life and has since from before time began. He inspires me to think more about the planet as a living being, to become more ecologically awake and responsible. His gratitude for the world, "so filled up with God," feels palpable, as does his commitment to a full, rich life of scholarship, service, ecological responsibility. Evolution is a forever ongoing process, suggests Art, and is the ongoing struggle of the Divine One toward creating intelligent and articulate life in humans. Prayer, he contends, can heal us, turn us toward wholeness, and tender life-giving energy to those for whom we pray.

When we are lost, Art suggests, when we cannot feel

a connection with the holiness of life, we need the reassurance of rituals, which we may find in our daily prayer books. Healing may also be seen as a path of individuation, so we can become the unique aspect of God that we are and then radiate our unique kind of love in our lives. All worship, he teaches, is giving and devotion, not asking. How grateful I am to read Art's suggestion that one of our greatest acts of humanization is the projection of the human image onto the Divine. I can stop feeling immature when I personify my prayer to my God. Art's beautiful work feels like God's face shining on me, especially when he asks, "Who is the projection of whom?"

Melila Hellner-Eshed – One of God's Faces

This is the Divine
as the great wellspring
of life, love, and forgiveness.
This face radiates
light, floods
over its banks, gushes
with vitality, and sustains
all things that come
into contact with it.
In its luminescence, being
itself becomes
possible.

It does not act, it simply
is.

Melila Hellner-Eshed and I connected immediately when we met on one of Alan's and my trips to Israel, where she lives. Her experience of the Divine, like mine, is visceral, intuitive, immediate. She describes God as the "beautiful dark light of Shekhinah" (*A River Flows from Eden*, p. 270). To meet God, she suggests, we sometimes must connect with the earth, go down to the ground. As we walk on the way, we can move from an experience that is physical and emotional back into the world of language and thought. Any connection with Melila, in person or when reading her work, is an invitation to become immersed in a world of wonder and the mystical, the poetic, the mythic, and the experiential. We meet the heroes of the Zohar as they arouse us to open our eyes, to awaken from slumber and immerse ourselves in life.

One purpose of mystical life, Melila suggests, is *tikkun ha-olam*, the healing of the world. She feels awe, daily, at the immense presence of the Holy. The Divine is changing all the time, she notes, as is life. If we are plugged in, we notice this. She speaks of the spectacular experience of life, movement, and beauty that has occurred, and does, so many times in her life. And when, Melila says, she has a particularly intense immersion in life's sacredness, when she feels she is in the presence of the Divine, she has the language of Judaism and the Zohar to help ground and expand her.

Melila and I talk with each other about dreams, the night gifts from the Beloved. We share wonder at the many ways the Holy One makes Godself known. We both have the awesome experience of sensing the divine spark within the people we encounter. She trusts her experience and encourages me to trust mine. My dream of walking into my room, she suggested, was a rite of passage. We learn that there is no light but that which emerges from darkness. We spoke of the terror of facing all I did in this intense time, and we celebrated my ecstasy and gratitude. In one beautiful conversation, Melila told me, "Remember that weeping is the next step. Melting. Streaming forth. Flowing, the darkness dissolves. And then again. More weeping."

In spending time with Melila, we come closer to the profound secrets of the Divine, to the source of utter love. In her book *Seekers of the Face*, she narrates the story of an emergency assembly convened by the hero of the Zohar. "The gathering," she recounts, "takes place in a field, among the trees, at a time beyond time and in a place beyond place" (*Seekers of the Face*, p. 1). The mission? To heal the face of God and thereby heal and transform the face of religion.

Lawrence Kushner — Who* Created These (*Mi Vara Ayleh*)

In the Holy of Holies, the snow geese,
cranes and great blue herons land
in the waters of the Bosque,
and, come first light, they fly away—
whether we are there to watch them,
or not.

Year after year they do it,
just as the great whales move
through the waters of the sea,
and mitochondria swim through
the fluid within our cells.

Everywhere, these great, flowing
streams of life are all doing
what they are meant to do—
one great orchestrated flow of life.

Who (Mi) one of the seventy-two names of God.

The Light of God's Shadow

Creation is a world of secrets, latent with layers of mysteries, suggests Lawrence Kushner. When Larry was a boy, art was his passion. But when he became a rabbi, his energy was expended in his rabbinate, writing, and the sharing of his spiritual teachings. At the age of sixty-seven, he suddenly knew he had to return to art, and began painting rural landscapes and cityscapes—the daily world he lovingly inhabits. Every painting is unmistakably shot through with the light that he sees as a metaphor for consciousness. "As an artist," he told me, "the only things that seem worthy of recording are what happens to them in the light or, if I can find a way, to simply record the light itself."

Though drawn to the light, Larry is insistent about including the dark side in his reflections on the Divine. Since everything is God, we don't have free choice, he contends. "The more we become aware," he teaches, "the more we realize that we are in everything, and everything is in us. The One we call the Holy One, and the ones the Holy One calls us, are the same beings, seen from different sides" (*River of Light*, p. 72).

Once or twice, Larry gave me a Jewish Zen slap, helping me know that when I try to seek control, I lose touch with primary sensibilities. He speaks about how God is trying to become conscious through humans, through suffering and beauty, through human pathos and kindness. If we do good things, we make more light.

I asked what he feels his number one teaching is, and Larry said it could be on a bumper sticker: IT'S YOUR EGO, STUPID. "Being conscious and intensely awake is the closest we come to God," he said, "but then we need to be ego-less, without an awareness of ourselves. Follow the living spirit and see where it leads you. Serendipity is God, too. Everything is."

Larry learns from everybody and everything. He believes

that what we need to do is concentrate on loving. When we emerge from an experience of beauty, we are closer to wholeness. "Even a worm is serving God, in its worming behavior," he said. He reminded me that the older you are, the more you know you are not in control. I asked him about *shmutz* cleaning. "Every day," Larry said, he pays attention to his *mishegas* (craziness). "And you can't get rid of it," he chuckled. We talk about how, from God's perspective, the past, present, and future all happen simultaneously. But since we cannot handle that, we filter it down to one thing at a time.

FOR FURTHER LEARNING

If you would like to read more of these teachers' works, I recommend my two favorites by each one.

Sanford Drob
Symbols of the Kabbalah: Philosophical and Psychological Perspectives
Kabbalistic Visions: C. G. Jung and Jewish Mysticism

Tirzah Firestone
Wounds into Wisdom: Healing Intergenerational Jewish Trauma
The Receiving: Reclaiming Jewish Women's Wisdom

Michael Fishbane
Sacred Attunement: A Jewish Theology
Fragile Finitude: A Jewish Hermeneutical Theology

Arthur Green
Judaism for the World: Reflections on God, Life, and Love
Seek My Face: A Jewish Mystical Theology

Melila Hellner-Eshed
A River Flows from Eden: The Language of Mystical Experience in the Zohar
Seekers of the Face: Secrets of the Idra Rabba (the Great Assembly) of the Zohar

Lawrence Kushner
Kabbalah: A Love Story
The River of Light: Jewish Mystical Awareness

Who Are Your Six?

ACKNOWLEDGEMENTS

The word *ubuntu*, from the Nguni languages of Zulu and Xhosa in South Africa, has a few meanings. They are all related to humanity and decency, concern about others. My favorite interpretation of the word *ubuntu*, though, is simply this: "I am who I am because of you."

Deep spiritual awakening is always both personal—a deepening journey—and collective. We exist in relationship to others. How we relate to our brothers and sisters, our mothers and fathers, is of paramount importance. I am fascinated by the lemniscate, which is a fancy name for the symbol of infinity. I like to conceive of deep connection as something that flows between two or more people. When I talk or listen to one of the wonderful people in my life, I often find my hand tracing the symbol of infinity, back and forth, back and forth—the energy of spirit moving between us.

Meet My Three Editors

When our creative work is touched by another and challenged honestly and lovingly, our hearts may begin to sing. Meet Emily Wichland, my prose editor, and Jason Ranek and Cathy Smith Bowers, my poetry mentors, all of whom helped me groan less and sing more, who helped me hear what was awakening in me.

Emily had been inviting me to write prose for many years. When it seemed that the Boss was on her side and I had no choice, we began working and growing together, and continued for the four years since the inception of this book. Emily's patience and humor were a tonic, as the book, which kept changing shape, became a forest and not just a whole bunch of trees. Emily's sparkling spirit, her capacity for wonder, and the delight she experiences in life, were balm to me during our four years of work together, especially when I was beset by more painful challenges than I had ever known. I told Emily that she and the Divine were the spiritual directors for this book. Spiritual directors help people listen to their souls. The book transformed me, and I live now with more equanimity and more love than I ever thought possible. There are no words to explain, describe, or understand how the energy of creation and awakening moved between Emily and me, and transformed us both. No words, just exquisite gratitude.

I must note that as synchronicity (God) would have it, all my editors are of the Christian faith. I rather love that this book, so suffused with Jewish mysticism, has been birthed with the help of three Christian midwives, one of whom is a man.

Emily was raised Catholic but does not identify with Catholicism. She says, "I don't identify with any religion, really. Religion as the business side of spirituality eventually goes bad—all that clamoring for market share can't but call to our human thirst for power and greed. I'm open to learning from the spiritual teachings of all spiritual traditions. And though I am not a joiner by nature, I enjoy experiencing spiritual community and ritual. I understand the wisdom that says you won't go deep by digging many shallow holes. But I see my spiritual quest as digging one big hole with whatever tools seem useful."

I was also extremely fortunate to have two such gifted, imaginative poets as mentors. Jason Ranek and Cathy Smith Bowers helped me hear what the poems, which sometimes arrived tangled up, were telling me. They spun me around with their workshopping and helped me turn my musings into

Acknowledgements

language that had me sighing in gratitude. Poems often took flight in their magical hands, returning to nest in the book. So grateful for the gift of their poetic visions, I was also blessed by the relationships of great mutuality and caring that developed with each of them.

Jason says, "I was raised Catholic in a devout Midwestern American family. At sixteen, after encountering Buddhism, I began a spiritual journey that culminated in my formally becoming a Pure Land Buddhist in 2008, which is where my tent remains pitched to this day. Recently, I have completed a book of divinatory poems based upon statues in the sculpture garden of Vigeland Park, in Oslo, Norway. Asking questions, casting the die, and receiving numbers that correspond to a statue and its accompanying poem, are all powerful, revelatory experiences. The archetypal statues are mainly social constellations of men, women, and children."

Cathy says, "My family was Baptist, very erratically orthodox Baptist. I consider myself Christian because I try to live by the lessons that Jesus taught on how we should treat other people. I pray all the time—mostly prayers of gratitude and invocations for forgiveness and guidance. Most of the time I find that I am talking to myself—and that's just fine. My religious discipline now includes regular sessions with a spiritual director, writing and teaching poetry, practicing yoga, gardening, and being present for family, friends, and strangers whose paths I might cross."

Readers, Friends, and Sisters

I am profoundly grateful for the people who read the whole book or parts of it during its gestation and as it was coming into final shape. They all "got it," and were interested, patient, enthusiastic. Their caring and honest feedback was enormously supportive and encouraging. I also talked endlessly about "the book," and almost always said some version of "The book is not the book, you know. It is one of God's primary ways of helping me wake up more. For now." Thank you to my readers, Judy Viorst, Rabbi Ed Elkin, Terry Hershey, Kristen Hobby, Diane Millis, Seifu Singh-Morales, Anna Miransky, Susie Kaufman, Alan Hoffmann.

I do spiritual friendship exchanges once a month with Laura Goldman, Susie Kaufman, Pam Lauer, David Liedl, Avruhm Addison, Bobbi Breitman. Like me, all are spiritual directors. We each take half an hour and talk, always listening for the wisdom that wants to be born in the sacred space around and between us. Think lemniscate. I am so grateful for the love, tenderness, laughter, and wisdom that I receive from each of them. They help me become more of who I am meant to be. Think *ubuntu*.

There are no words to express my love for my sisters, Vicki Davidoff, who lives in British Columbia, and Sue Davidoff, who lives in Cape Town South Africa. We all know how unresolved family-of-origin wounds can create messy and painful feelings and relationships. We sisters have had to work through some "stuff" over the years. Doing so has resulted in remarkable and honest closeness and very deep love. The book was written during the period when I was in trouble more often than not. Vicki and Sue loved me, listened endlessly to my heart, and even made me feel, sometimes, that I was being brave. They continue to companion me in the deeply reflective and spiritual aspects of my life, as well as in the everyday delights and challenges.

Acknowledgements

Those I Companion

Over the years I have been most fortunate to companion a number of people in psychotherapy and spiritual direction. It is a great privilege to hold the space while the person before me listens deeply to what is calling them from their depths. All intentional waking-up practices are authored by mystery. When two or more sit together and listen carefully, everyone is enriched and transformed. Even during the times when, in my room, I was scraping my bones together, I felt nourished by the sessions. Plus, most of the time, my people, as I refer to them, are wildly interesting and often funny and delightful.

Family

Family. How does anyone ever write adequate words about what is most soul-important? Alan and I started our story in the mid-sixties by holding hands when we should not have. Now in 2021, there is a family that is so large we would need to rent a midsize hotel if we had a reunion. Our sons, Eli, Glen, and Daniel were born to us. You have read many times about our beloved Eli, and the holes his death has left in us. You have also met Glen and Daniel—such beautiful men—and their beloved families: their wives Medina and Terri, and the two girls each family has, Maya, Clara, Ayla and Hannah. And beloved Ilana, Eli's widow, now mother and father to fifteen children, some of whom have their own children. Think twelve great-grands for Alan and me. We are remarkably close to all our family, and the times we spend with them are lively, loving, and frequently enormous fun. We miss our Israeli family terribly.

How do I thank Alan? He has been in my heart since I was

seventeen. So different from me, he yet meets me in all the important ways, and listens to all I want to talk about, and talk I do. He has read several incarnations of this book and engaged in endless discussions with me. Kind and patient when I have said, "This is it!" he knows enough not to bet money on what the book will ultimately say. You have met Alan in many of the poems and stories. Quite separate from all the ways Alan has helped me with the book and my life, he is also an unusual, interesting, enjoyable, enormously capable man. We also have fun every single day. You know that he is the love of my life and is also occasionally the bane of it. Light and dark. This book is all about that.

Family is the ballast for my life and my heart. So many words, I usually have. Here, I am reduced to being a bumbling idiot.

ABOUT THE AUTHOR

Jennifer (Jinks) Hoffmann, poetry editor for Spiritual Directors International, was born in South Africa but has lived in Canada since 1966. Originally a Speech Therapist, Jinks is now a Spiritual Director and Psychotherapist. Jinks has had a book of poetry published (*It's All God, Anyway*) and has had many poems published in books, journals and on-line. A devotee of waking up for over forty years, Jinks reads, writes, walks, works with her dreams, and pays attention to her daily messes and triumphs—ever in search of Mystery, all the while knowing that Mystery is searching for her.

Made in the USA
Monee, IL
02 November 2023

45619823R00198